# Praise for The Jc

"Dr. Joseph is a trailblazer who has created a leading-edge visualization system for recovery and reemployment. No job seeker should be without it."

— Mark Victor Hansen, co creator, the bestselling *Chicken Soup for the Soul* series, co author, *The One Minute Millionaire*

"The Job-Loss Recovery Program is consistently praised by our corporate and individual clients. It helps shorten the time from layoff to employment. Lynn Joseph demystifies the process for even the most doubtful user through clear and practical instructions."

— Murray A. Mann, Principal, Global Diversity Solutions Group, LLC and co author, Barron's *The Complete Job Search Guide for Latinos*

"I cannot recommend *The Job-Loss Recovery Program Guide* more highly. Dr. Lynn Joseph is truly a pioneer in the fields of psychology and career development. In this highly readable volume, she shows compassion and genuine concern about the lives of people in career transition. Moreover, her book reflects these qualities with both warmth and scientific objectivity . . . In addition, the Guide highlights excellent tools and exercises to get results fast!"

— Marky Stein, bestselling author of *Fearless Interviewing: How to Win the Job by Communicating With Confidence*, www.markystein.com

"I ordered both the book and CD to try out the visualization exercises and the impact was amazing in my job search. I went through each of the six exercises and each time would see a spike in my job search activities ... I wound up in the job of my dreams with (honestly!) the salary I desired, a nice increase from my previous position! I really credit the JLRPG in helping out tremendously in that process! What a blessing! Thank you!"

— Helen Galletly, Career Coach

"A big thank you for the powerful work you are doing. Benefits the JLR Program gave me:

- Deeper Relaxation
- Emotional Release. I can focus on the now again.
- Possibilities. I was reminded again of the possibilities that exist and that my potential is still unfolding.
- New Strength. In the interviewing script I discovered a strength that I have never articulated before...
- Future Self. It is as if my perspective is changing to her perspective day by day. Really powerful!"

— Erica Hamilton, Manager, Financial Services

"This program of imagery-based exercises offers six sessions to help overcome the stress, grief, and anger of job loss; and to improve interview performance, boost confidence, & engender a positive attitude, so a new job can be found. This is a beautifully written and spoken program of high quality materials that will help a person move on in the best possible way."

> — Belleruth Naparstek, creator of the Health Journeys guided imagery audio series, author of *Invisible Heroes*

"Lynn's work in job loss recovery is stand-alone. There is nothing like it. It addresses a piece of work that doesn't often get addressed and that is a significant barrier to moving forward - our feelings. This is not band-aid work or surface work. Lynn's understanding of the full experience in career transition is very timely."

> — Eileen Piersa, OD Consultant/Executive Coach/Career Transition Coach, Piersa Consulting

"People who have lost their jobs can feel profound fear and trepidation. Lynn Joseph's work is a true gift to them."

> — Marianne Williamson, author of the New York Times bestseller *A Return to Love*, and *The Age of Miracles: Embracing the New Midlife*

"The Job Loss Recovery Program Guide is a practical guide for using the power of visualization to recover from the trauma of job loss by making new body-mind-spirit connections. Dr. Lynn Joseph's step-by-step strategies are easy to follow and will help you move quickly toward success and healing."

> — Barbara M. Dossey, Ph.D., RN, Director, Holistic Nursing Consultants, Santa Fe, New Mexico, and author of *Rituals of Healing*

# The
# JOB-LOSS
# RECOVERY
## Program Guide
### The Ultimate Visualization System
### for Landing a Great Job Now


Lynn Joseph, Ph.D.


Discovery Dynamics Incorporated

Publisher's Note

*This publication is designed to provide accurate and authoritative information in regard to the subject matter covered. It is sold with the understanding that the publisher is not engaged in rendering psychological, financial, legal, or other professional services. If expert assistance or counseling is needed, the services of a competent professional should be sought.*

Discovery Dynamics' Web site address: www.discoverydynamics.net

Updated, enhanced edition of *The Job-Loss Recovery Guide: A Proven Program for Getting Back To Work—Fast!* (New Harbinger Publications, Inc., 2003)

# CONTENTS

Preface ................................................................................ix
Introduction ........................................................................ 1

# PART I

Laying the Foundation:
What This Program Will Do for You

## Chapter 1

Job Loss: A Traumatic Event ................................................ 9
  Stages and Symptoms of Job-Loss Grief
  Goals for a Quick Recovery
  How This Book Will Help You
  Level of Distress Questionnaire

## Chapter 2

Bounce Back with Guided Visualization ............................... 22
  What Is Guided Visualization?
  How Guided Visualization Is Used Today
  What Guided Visualization Can Do for You
  Make an Ally of Your Subconscious Mind
  How Confident Are You Right Now?
  The Three Levels of a Guided Visualization Experience
  The Power Tools of Manifestation
  Fringe Benefits

## Chapter 3

The Job-Loss Recovery Program ........................................... 38
  The Program's Foundation
  Guided Visualization Scripts and How to Use Them
  Program Structure
  How to Make the Most of Your Sessions
  No Experience Necessary

# PART II
## The Power of Closure: Module 1

**Chapter 4**

Relax and Create a Safe Place ...................................................47

Benefits of Relaxation

Script: Basic Relaxation Skills

**Chapter 5**

Mastering Distressing Emotions........................................51

Closure Is Critical

Four Steps to Emotional Mastery

**Chapter 6**

Meeting Your Successful Future Self ...................................59

Moving toward Your Future Self

Implementing Module 1

Module 1 Script Introduction

Alternate Program Structure

Module 1 Script: Relaxation, Emotional Closure, Meeting Your
    Future Self

After Completing Module 1

# Part III
## Getting the Job You Really Want: Module 2

**Chapter 7**

Rehearsing Your Success........................................................79

Improving Self-Confidence and Competence

**Chapter 8**

Meeting Your Mentor ............................................................83

Access Your Inner Wisdom

Develop New Insight through Reframing

Implementing Module 2

Module 2 Script Introduction

Module 2 Script: Relaxation, Mentally Rehearsing a Job
    Interview, Meeting Your Mentor

After Completing Module 2

**Chapter 9**

Breaking Your Barriers..........................................................98

    Quickly Identify and Change Limiting Beliefs

    Break Negative Emotional Contracts with Others

    Discover and Learn from Your Resistances

**Chapter 10**

Your New Vision:................................................................112

    Making a Living with No Emotional Barriers

    Review Your Accomplishments

    Create a New Vision for Your Life

**Appendix A**

Guided Visualization Scripts:.............................................114

    Individual Program Scenarios

**Appendix B**

Supplemental Exercises......................................................122

**Appendix C**

References ........................................................................127

# Preface

This second edition of *The Job-Loss Recovery Guide* is especially important and meaningful, given the worldwide economic meltdown that began in the last quarter of 2008.

A new economic landscape is emerging. Our personal lives reflect this financial upheaval. Just as financial institutions must reinvent and restructure themselves, so too do individuals need to rethink their positions in the job market.

But positive transformation can transcend this startling change. We can create our capabilities of doing and becoming. Now is the time to step out of our former limited self images and consciously create new images with expanded boundaries. The world actually demands new skill sets and extended ranges of possibilities.

Once upon a time people looked at creative visualization as a flight of fancy and a desperate measure for desperate people. Well, it just isn't so anymore. Olympic coaches, highly trained and successful athletes such as golf great Tiger Woods and Olympic swimming star Michael Phelps, and corporate mavericks all know that you can't create success before you can imagine it. Moreover, the science of quantum physics now tells us that our desires, expectations, and imagination are potent tools of manifestation and our bodies are actually energy in motion, highly impacted by our thoughts and feelings.

So here's what I'd like to do together with you. Let's be willing to step outside the bounds of who you think you are and what you think you can do. And most of all let's restock your toolbox with the ultimate visualization system to help you land the job you really want now!

# Introduction

At age fifty-one, Rick was abruptly laid off from his job of three years as a manager in Systems and Technology. He entered my job-loss recovery study two months into a frustrating job search. Immediately following the study, Rick wrote, "I was very fortunate to be a member of your study group . . . and I will always appreciate it. Your program addressed inner control and understanding, while allowing me to move past the emotional side of being laid off."

Less than two months later, Rick accepted a new position as a senior project manager; however, he emailed me eight months into his new job to say, "The company I went to work for has started major downsizing. My project and my entire department are being out-sourced to India. This is business, and change is part of the game. Rest assured your program will help me address the challenge ahead."

Downsizing was no longer just a temporary phenomenon. Corporate downsizing and restructuring had become common strategies designed to reduce expenses and increase profits and had resulted in significant employee displacement and transition. Exiting (or displaced) employees everywhere would need new tools to quickly take control of their careers. I was certain I could provide those tools.

## Where I'm Coming From

Let me back up a bit. When, in the third year of my doctoral studies, it became necessary to select a research topic for my dissertation, I gravitated toward a subject that had held my interest for many years: guided visualization technology. Guided visualization—you may also know it as creative visualization or guided imagery—is a thought process that consciously directs and focuses the imagination to create an internal experience. It includes the use of all five senses for maximum effectiveness: sight, sound, touch, taste, and smell.

Positive change, healing, and goal achievement can all happen more quickly with the use of guided visualization than without it. I knew this to be true from the research I'd done on the techniques, and from having experienced its seeming magic in my own life.

Once I selected my doctoral research topic, I needed an application on which to test it. I ultimately chose reemployment for three reasons.

- If guided visualization were found effective in reducing landing time after job loss, many people could conceivably benefit.

- The test of guided visualization effectiveness would seem more credible and practical in a real-world environment than in a laboratory.

- I felt I could be successful in recruiting participants for the study since I had worked for many years in corporate America and related well to businesspeople.

My initial motivation, then, was to test and hopefully demonstrate the effectiveness of guided visualization in promoting reemployment for business people who had been laid off.

I later learned that exiting employees often moved through the stages of grief most commonly experienced after the loss of a loved one: shock and denial; fear, anxiety, anger; bargaining; depression; and finally acceptance. In the case of the unemployed, researchers call it "job-loss grief." If you have lost your job, you may be familiar with some or all of these grieving stages. You should understand that your feelings are normal, and that this book will show you how to manage and move through them quickly by using the guided visualization career-transition program I created for that purpose. It has proven to be quick and easy to use and has helped many exiting employees recover and get back to work fast. The entire program can be completed in just six daily sessions of about twenty minutes each.

## Where We're Going

*The Job-Loss Recovery Program Guide* is divided into three parts. Part 1 lays the foundation by describing the symptoms and stages of grief that may accompany your job loss and explaining the guided visualization that will help you recover. It also provides the structure of the Job-Loss Recovery Program.

You'll get a good understanding of the guided visualization that supports this program, what it is, what it can do for you, and its program components, which I call scenarios because each is a scripted experience. I describe the program's organizational structure, which includes the six guided visualization sessions mentioned.

Part 2 takes you step-by-step through Sessions 1, 2, and 3, in which you will resolve the loss, boost your self-esteem, and improve your job-search motivation and performance.

Part 3 guides you through Sessions 4, 5, and 6, in which you will increase your self-confidence and further enhance your job-search competence. I will guide you through each of the six sessions.

*The Job-Loss Recovery Program Guide* will teach you how to break through the barriers that may impede success and how to create a new vision for your life. In short, you can discover in these pages the tools and resources to find success within yourself. You'll not only achieve reemployment success, but I believe you'll want to use these tools to improve your life every day.

## Changing Loyalties and New Identities

You are not alone. Millions of employee layoffs have resulted from the global financial crisis with its resulting recession, bringing about enormous and far-reaching casualties. It's not surprising that we live in an age of anxiety, and fear that we may not be able to take care of our families.

This book will help you develop calmness and clarity, and help you reduce your landing time significantly. Employees have, traditionally, obtained their sense of identity and self-esteem from the organization. If you want to develop a more authentic and lasting sense of identity and self-esteem, however, you must stop defining yourself in relation to your business organization. Instead, connect with a personal core purpose, awaken your spirit, gain control over your life, and engage in work that reflects your ideal self. If you believe this is out of reach for you, now is a good time to consider stretching that belief. I'm convinced that you can achieve each of these goals using the guided visualization program and the techniques I share with you in *The Job-Loss Recovery Program Guide.*

## *Transforming Trauma to Triumph: How Science Supports This Book*

People often ask me about the Job-Loss Recovery Program's underlying study, so I will give you a brief summary. If you'd like to read the published academic article in its entirety, it is referenced at the end of this book under L. M. Joseph and M. A. Greenberg.

Fifty-two professional men and women who had been laid off— primarily managers and executives—volunteered for the study. The overall objective was to compare the effectiveness of a career-transition program to a placebo control protocol in promoting reemployment. Most of us think of a sugar pill when we hear or see the word "placebo," but, in this case, placebo refers to the test condition that participants incorrectly believe is the effective condition being tested.

In this study, for example, participants were randomly assigned to two groups. Participants in each group received six sessions of a twenty-minute visualization protocol designed to make them believe it would facilitate their job search. But only one group received the career-transition program visualizations.

Participants in the career-transition program group listened to a recording of my voice reading a visualization script designed to help them achieve closure, improve motivation and job-search competence, and increase confidence. Participants in the placebo control group followed written instructions to sit silently while visualizing themselves executing current job-search plans for half of each twenty-minute session; and, for the remaining half, visualizing future job-search plans.

The result of the study was astonishing: two months after their sessions, five times more participants in the career-transition program group had begun full-time, permanent work than had the placebo control group participants. It's unusual in academic research to find such a large difference between groups. As an added bonus to the study results, participants who accepted jobs within two months did not suffer a decrease in salary. The program worked well and it worked fast, as I'd hoped. The graph below shows the results.

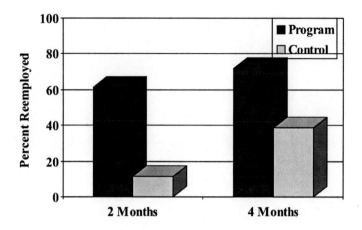

Participants in the study ranged in age from twenty-nine to sixty-four, with an average age of forty-seven, and almost two-thirds were back to work in two months or less, following the program.

You can be, too.

You may want to designate a specific notebook or journal as your Job-Loss Recovery Journal. It will be useful to track your progress and to make notes as you complete the suggested exercises.

I wrote this book as mainly a guide and workbook to accompany the audio CD titled *The Job-Loss Recovery Program: The Ultimate Visualization System for Landing a Great Job Now!* It is also appropriate for independent use, as all guided visualization scripts are included to either read or record for your own playback. If, like many people, you prefer to use professionally recorded scripted exercises, the audio CD is for you. My voice, accompanied by Celtic harpist Lisa Lynne, gently guides you through each transformational scripted exercise. See page 131 for more information.

# PART I

## Laying the Foundation: What This Program Will Do for You

# Chapter 1

## *Job Loss: A Traumatic Event*

*People are like stained-glass windows. They sparkle and shine when the sun is out, but when darkness sets in, their true beauty is revealed only if there is a light from within.*
—Elisabeth Kubler-Ross

Standing in his boss's office, forty-five-year-old Paul felt as if he'd just had the wind knocked out of him. He'd been laid off after ten years of loyal service.

How would his family survive? He received some company severance pay and had put aside a little money for emergencies. But it wouldn't last long.

In the ensuing weeks, Paul had trouble sleeping and concentrating and often felt depressed. He blamed himself for having lost his job. He wondered if he had worked harder and for longer hours, whether he'd have been let go. But deep down he knew he'd been a good worker. He felt humiliated, abandoned, and betrayed by his company.

Paul's reaction is common, and his fear and anxiety are justified. Studies show, at his age, finding another job may take over five months in a "normal" economic environment.

Typically, severance pay is one week's salary per year of service. This means the average manager with five years' tenure would receive only five weeks' salary on termination. Even Paul's ten weeks' severance pay clearly won't support a five-month job search. And surveys indicate that when managers and professionals are rehired after being laid off, they often earn 20 to 30 percent less than in their previous positions.

Psychologists recognize job loss as one of life's most traumatic experiences. It's a stressful, life-changing event—one that can lead to negative mental and physical health consequences and jeopardize financial security and family relationships.

According to research results by Price, Choi, and Vinokur (2002), unemployment can start a vicious cycle of depression, loss of personal control, decreased emotional functioning, and poorer physical health. They concluded this from interviewing 756 recently unemployed job seekers over two years. At the end of the two years, 71 percent were re-employed, working at least 20 hours or more per week, but *still reported the negative effects of their job loss.*

Soon after the terrorist attacks of September 11, 2001, Georgia Witkin, Ph.D., Assistant Clinical Professor of Psychiatry and Director of the Stress Program at the Mount Sinai School of Medicine in New York City, gave a stress-relief workshop to 1500 employees of the Syosset, Long Island, School District. Many of the employees were in shock and grieving for their lost loved ones and neighbors while simultaneously trying to help their students overcome fear and anger.

The group was asked to write down their most stressful experience before the terrorist attacks. Then they were asked to rate that experience on a scale of one (lowest stress) to ten (highest stress), and then to rate their stress from the terrorist attacks on the same scale. To the surprise of Dr. Witkin and the researchers at the Stress Program, although the horrible terrorist trauma received relevantly high stress ratings, the personal traumas and losses got even higher stress ratings. Dr. Witkin concluded that, clearly, no disaster is small if the loss is personal.

Therefore, please do not minimize the personal impact of your job loss. It is absolutely normal for you and your family to feel a great deal of stress.

You may want to pause for a moment to rate your job-loss stress on a scale of one to ten. What number came to mind? As a comparison, the stress rating for the September eleventh disaster averaged 7.8 stress points.

The loss of your job requires coping efforts. In this context, "coping" means the process of managing the stressful situation and the emotions that situation brings up. How you perceive, appraise, and cope with the loss will then largely determine how quickly you recover. Your appraisal will determine why and to what degree a situation is stressful.

There is a widely held myth that our thoughts are a result of our feelings. You would first feel frightened, for instance, and then mentally appraise the situation as frightening. In truth, it most often works in reverse; that is, you first think the situation is frightening, and then you feel frightened. Accordingly, if you change your thoughts about the situation, your feelings will also change.

The Job-Loss Recovery Program in this book will help you improve your coping skills and shift your thoughts, assisting you to appraise your job-loss situation more rationally and productively as a challenge rather than a threat.

John F. Kennedy once said, "When written in Chinese, the word 'crisis' is composed of two characters—one represents danger and the other represents opportunity." I hope you'll recognize the hidden opportunity in your current situation. Though it may not seem like it at the moment, your experience of it is really a matter of perspective.

Along with helping you to develop your inner management skills, this tested and proven program is designed to put you back in control of your career, so when you take the actions necessary to get back to work, you'll be far more successful, far more quickly.

## Stages and Symptoms of Job-Loss Grief

If you are a casualty of corporate downsizing, merging, or restructuring, understand that it's normal for you to have symptoms and emotions such as the following:

| | |
|---|---|
| Shame | Loss of confidence |
| Fear | Sadness |
| Anxiety | Depression |
| Sense of abandonment and betrayal | Feelings of failure |
| Anger | Loneliness |
| Guilt | Irritability |
| Depression | Loss of appetite |
| Loss of self-esteem | Trouble sleeping |
| | Bad dreams |

The list is long and may seem intimidating. In fact, this section about the stages and symptoms of job-loss grief may feel a little discouraging. Yet, the first step on the path of healing is to recognize and own what you're feeling. Only then can you resolve those feelings and begin to take back control of your life.

Research tells us that the strongest predictors of negative reactions to job loss are financial distress and attachment to the previous job. In other words, the more stress you feel over meeting financial demands or the more involved you were in your last job, the more distressed you are likely to feel. Your initial reaction may be to hold back any heavy emotions and get on with your job search.

Yet, by stuffing your uncomfortable thoughts and feelings, you can put yourself at greater risk for negative results, including illness. At the very least, this inhibition can reduce your ability to mentally work through many aspects of the stressful event, which results in your distressing thoughts and feelings just getting worse.

So you can see how denying, avoiding, or feeling guilty about your feelings is really counterproductive to healing—and to conducting a successful job search. You simply need to take the time to grieve.

Many authorities, including the late, renowned authority on death and dying, Elisabeth Kubler-Ross, explain unemployment as a trauma that induces reactions similar to the loss of a loved one or to facing terminal illness, an experience that requires a period of grieving. Dr. Kubler-Ross recognized and formulated the stages of grieving most people experience after the loss of a loved one (1969, 1997).

> Shock and denial
>
> Fear and anxiety
>
> Anger
>
> Bargaining
>
> Depression
>
> Acceptance

The stages have been widely documented to apply to job loss, as well. Losing a job can initiate some or all of these stages, and they can be experienced in any order.

In *Career Bounce-Back* (1998), J. Damian Birkel has modified these stages to more accurately reflect the job-loss grief process he calls The "emotional wave" (or "e-wave," for short). According to the e-wave model, when you hear you've been terminated, you are thrown into an ocean of emotional waves.

As you begin the climb up one wave, you are first in the shock and denial stage, followed by the fear and anxiety stage. As you move up the crest of the wave, you pass through the stages of anger, bargaining, depression, and finally the trough of the wave and what Birkel calls "temporary acceptance." It's temporary because, unlike Kubler-Ross's more permanent acceptance stage following the death of a loved one, you will cycle through many more waves before you learn to confront and manage your e-wave emotions. At that point, you can safely reach the shore.

Remember though, you may not even experience all of the stages. On the other hand, you may cycle through some of the stages more than once. Let's take a closer look at one client's journey through each of the stages. You may recognize your own feelings in his story.

Richard, a thirty-eight-year-old accountant and department manager, experienced his layoff notification a little differently than Paul. When he first heard about his job termination, he thought, "This can't be happening to me. It happens to other people, not me. They'll find out they made a mistake and call me back."

Richard had experienced the shock and denial stage. Numbness set in.

Shock and numbness are the body-mind's ways of allowing us to function on automatic pilot—without interference from distressing emotions—for a few hours after any traumatic event. Nothing seems real, and you feel detached. In fact, you may not feel the full impact of your job loss for days or even weeks.

When Richard broke the news to his family, he sensed the fear they tried to hide behind a stoic front. He then began to realize the reality of his situation and moved into the fear and anxiety stage, where he stayed for several weeks. Since he had lost control of his career, he began to lose confidence in himself. His thoughts raced from, "I haven't had to look for a job in years," to "What if no employer wants me?" on to "I could lose everything."

Richard felt abandoned and betrayed by his company because so much that he valued had been taken away from him. He felt intolerably vulnerable.

Panic emerged and, as he feared the worst, small issues began to take on overwhelming importance. At this point, he could easily have become immobilized.

Richard felt he'd been a loyal, hard-working employee and deserved better than a pink slip. He'd been dealt a serious blow that he experienced as an injustice. But, unfortunately, he hadn't allowed himself the anger that was his right. Rather than experience the anger stage, he unconsciously turned his wrath inward and instead became depressed, skipping right over the bargaining stage. He began thinking he deserved to lose his job, that it was his fault, and that he should have known enough to circulate his resume long before his layoff.

I'd like you to bear in mind that when you direct anger at yourself (such as Richard did when he blamed himself for being laid off), you set up a downward-spiral pattern that can lead to depression and immobility—not what you need to move forward productively.

Four months into his job search, with severance pay long gone and little savings left, Richard began bargaining with God: "If you help me find a job, I'll never take it for granted again."

Richard's wife sensed his desperation and felt helpless. She then saw an article about my career-transition program and encouraged him to contact me. He did.

Once Richard managed to resolve his feelings and to evaluate his situation more positively, he felt closure on his past job and progressed to the acceptance stage. That important step paved the way for him to clearly and aggressively focus on getting the job he wanted. Soon after he completed the program, he received and accepted a good offer from a company he had targeted. But he had to come to terms with his feelings—to let himself grieve—before he could put his energy fully toward his search.

## Goals for a Quick Recovery

A key goal of the Job-Loss Recovery Program, then, is to help you move quickly through the stages of grieving to a once-and-for-all acceptance with closure. But other important goals follow that one. For example, you might very well have damaged confidence and self-esteem, as well as other anxiety-producing feelings related to gaining reemployment. These issues also need to be addressed.

Thus, this program was designed to help you achieve each of the following goals for a quick recovery:

- Learn to relax and manage your stress.

- Process and resolve any distressing emotional reactions.

- Boost your confidence and self-esteem.

- Improve job-search competence.

- Take control of your future.

- Renew and maintain hope.

- Land the job of your choice.

The first goal is to manage your stress by learning to relax. You will be guided through an exercise to reduce external distractions, slow your breathing, and decrease muscle tension, which will result in greater calm and more-focused thinking. All of your program sessions will be preceded by this relaxation exercise and will be more effective as a result.

When you leave negative feelings unexpressed and unprocessed, you may unintentionally block your success in the job search. In fact, research has shown emotional expression to be effective in promoting reemployment. Therefore, the second goal is to resolve any distressing feelings and fully accept the employment termination. This will enhance your motivation and promote a successful job search as you apply this new, positive attitude to organizing, assimilating, and finding meaning in the event. In other words, you will then reach closure on that part of your past.

In one layoff study, exit interviews were taped with forty-seven exiting employees (LaFarge 1994). All felt ambivalent about leaving their companies and colleagues. They vacillated between wanting to stay while feeling righteous anger toward the organization for terminating them and wanting to leave the job and company behind. They described separation grief as painful. Yet, they had mixed feelings about letting go of the grief because it was their last connection with the company. Many also fluctuated between trying to justify the corporate actions and condemning those same hurtful actions.

Interestingly—and this may apply to you—most were unaware of their ambivalence. The more immediate needs of finding a new job and explaining things to friends and family were given precedence over exploring their own emotions. The researchers concluded that this failure to recognize and explore mixed feelings contributed to their difficulty in accepting and moving on and could, in addition, contribute to a delayed emotional investment in a new organization.

The displaced workers felt uncomfortable emotions yet, at the same time, recognized the opportunities for growth. Coping with these vacillating feelings that resulted in anxiety became one of the most difficult tasks they faced in resolving their trauma.

> # EXPRESSING EMOTIONS SAFELY PROMOTES REEMPLOYMENT.

Many of the former employees in the same investigation also fluctuated between feelings of competence and powerlessness. They wanted to believe in their competence, and cited many examples to support this belief, while, at the same time, the layoff had made many of them feel unsure of themselves and of their ability to function effectively.

Another interesting study tested the effects of written emotional expression—also called "emotional disclosure"—on obtaining reemployment success. Spera, Buhrfeind, and Pennebaker (1994) conducted the study with sixty-three professional participants (mostly engineers). The group's average age was fifty-four and they had been with their former employer an average of twenty years. All were recruited at an outplacement firm following a large-scale layoff from their company.

Participants were assigned to either a disclosive writing group, a control writing group, or a nonwriting control group. The disclosive writing group wrote about their thoughts and feelings regarding their termination for twenty minutes a day, for five days. The control writing group wrote about non-traumatic topics and the nonwriting control group did not write at all.

Three months after the writing week, 25 percent of the participants in the disclosive writing group were employed, none of the writing control participants had success, and 9 percent of the nonwriting control participants had jobs. Thus, those who wrote about the trauma of losing their jobs were significantly more likely to find reemployment in the months following the study than those who did not.

The Job-Loss Recovery Program will guide you safely through an emotional-expression scenario that will occur in your mind rather than in writing. In addition, you'll be able to do the exercise in a way that's designed to promote resolution and closure. You'll learn more about that process in chapter 5.

Two other important goals for a quick recovery are to regain confidence through self-esteem and to improve job-search competence. The entire program is designed to boost your confidence, but nowhere will you benefit more than in the mental-rehearsal scenario where you will practice your interviewing skills. Mentally rehearsing job interviews will also improve your job-search performance. I explain mental rehearsal and its benefits in chapter 7.

Renewed self-esteem can provide a significant advantage in an interview, affecting how aggressively and persuasively you sell your job skills. In addition, high self-esteem is a quality sought after by most employers. In fact, many researchers have found a strong relationship between career success and positive self-esteem.

> ACCEPTING THE LOSS, MAINTAINING A POSITIVE ATTITUDE, AND FEELING IN CONTROL PROMOTE FASTER REEMPLOYMENT.

If you don't currently have the skills to conduct an effective job search and do not receive outplacement services, there are quite a number of resources that can help you out. For example, local workforce development centers often provide complimentary job-search skill-building workshops. Many good books are also available to help improve your skills in resume and letter writing, interviewing, and negotiating job offers. And a growing number of credentialed career coaches and counselors support clients in transition.

The fifth goal of the Job-Loss Recovery Program is to help you take control of your future. People's inability to prevent the loss of their job is typically felt as a loss of personal control, which conflicts with the wish we all have for power and mastery. You will be reminded throughout this book that you are in total control of your thoughts, feelings, and behaviors. As you move through the program, accepting the loss, planning the future, and rehearsing success, your sense of control and emotional mastery will develop and expand.

The sixth goal for a quick recovery is for you to maintain hope throughout the job search. Positive beliefs are a key forerunner to an effective search for reemployment. This program will help you to see job loss as a challenge to overcome, and as an experience from which you can learn and grow.

When you achieve the six goals above, the seventh—landing the job of your choice—should happen naturally. When you can honestly put the past behind, rebuild your confidence and self-esteem, perform competently in job-search activities, feel in control of your life, and think optimistically, you will find positive reemployment.

One more thing: take time to laugh. Laughter blocks anxiety and fear by releasing the body's stress-reducing biochemicals. Dr. Lin Morel writes in *Get Clear. Get Connected. Get a Job.* (2009) that laughter heals our hurts and soothes the soul. It also takes our minds off our troubles and gives our psyche a much needed rest. So go ahead and watch a funny movie with family and friends, read some good jokes, listen to a comic, or anything that tickles your funny bone.

## How This Book Will Help You

Your journey of growth has begun, and the first step along the path is opening this book. In these pages you will learn to quickly and easily take control of your career despite the emotional setback of job loss. You will empower yourself with new tools to heal wounds, to create success and happiness, and even to find meaning and purpose.

Does this sound miraculous? Maybe it does, depending on your perspective. The Random House Webster's College Dictionary (2001) defines a miracle as an event that surpasses known human powers or natural forces. The operative word is "known." Today, scientists know more about human potential than just a few years ago. They better understand how the mind and body work—and how they work together. What we previously thought was impossible now seems very possible.

> YOU WILL LEARN TO QUICKLY RESOLVE
> DISTRESSING EMOTIONS AND TAKE CONTROL
> OF YOUR CAREER.

I challenge you to put aside skepticism for the moment. Read this book and earnestly implement the program. After all, it's not that much of a sacrifice—the entire program can be completed in just six daily sessions of about twenty minutes each.

Here are some tips that will help you make the most of this book.

- Make the Job-Loss Recovery Program an integral part of your job search. Reserve a time for the sessions now in your daily planner.

- Complete the questionnaires honestly so you can track your emotional progress as you advance through the program.

- Actively engage in the additional exercises provided to improve your self-understanding and guided visualization skills. As your skills improve, your sessions will have an increasingly positive impact on your job search.

I will lead you through the entire process, as you resolve your most difficult feelings and improve job-search performance.

## Level of Distress Questionnaire

Please take a few minutes right now to complete the following Level of Distress Questionnaire. Don't put it off. It will help you identify the symptoms of stress that may interfere with your success. In an effort to cope with uncomfortable feelings, you may be suppressing them or pushing them aside, unaware of their potential impact on your job search.

I will be asking you to complete the questionnaire now, after your third program session, and when you have completed the sixth session. This repetition will enable you to track your return to emotional health, watching your distress score drop lower and lower. The final question reflects your sense of control over job loss. As you begin to feel more in control of your situation, your score will drop on that single statement as well.

The significance of your initial total score is relative. It simply reflects your level of distress and will be used only for comparison with your later scores as you advance through the program. There are no good or bad scores. You already know you're feeling stressed, or you wouldn't be reading this book. This questionnaire will help you to see your progress.

As stress-relief expert Dr. Witkin (2002) puts it, "We're built for emotional survival." You know you will get through this challenge. Make the choice to grow wiser, stronger, and more resilient as a result of it.

In chapter 2, I will explain guided visualization in more detail: how it's used today in several arenas, what it can do for you, and how this program can help you get back to work fast.

# Level of Distress Questionnaire

The statements listed below refer to your inner feelings in regard to your job loss. Using the following scale from 1 to 10, insert the number that most closely reflects your current feelings and state of mind.

| 1 | 2 | 3 | 4 | 5 | 6 | 7 | 8 | 9 | 10 |
|---|---|---|---|---|---|---|---|---|----|
| *Never* | | *Sometimes* | | | *Frequently* | | | *Most of the Time* | |

_____ I have trouble focusing on what I am doing.

_____ I feel anxious.

_____ I feel frustrated.

_____ I have waves of distressing feelings.

_____ I am reminded of my job loss often.

_____ I try to ignore my feelings about my job loss.

_____ I feel depressed.

_____ I have trouble staying motivated.

_____ I feel angry and/or resentful.

_____ I have trouble sleeping because I keep thinking about my job loss.

_____ I feel fearful.

_____ Any reminder brings back stressful feelings.

_____ I have troubling dreams about my job loss.

For this final statement, use a 1 to 10 scale but, this time, 1 indicates *Strongly Disagree* and 10 means *Strongly Agree*. Insert the number that most closely reflects your current belief, as is relevant to your job loss.

_____ Little can be done to change my job-related problems.

_____ **Total your score here.**

This score represents your current level of distress about your job loss and is for future comparison purposes only.

# Chapter 2
## *Bounce Back with Guided Visualization*

*A mind is like a parachute. It has to be open in order to work.*
—Frank Zappa

## *What Is Guided Visualization Technology?*

Guided visualization (also known as guided imagery) directs and focuses the mind and imagination to achieve mental, physical, and emotional goals for health, well-being, and success. The process involves all five senses: sight, sound, smell, taste, and touch. Typically, you are guided to confront and let go of any worries, fears, or challenges.

You may practice visualizing alone, with guidance from a coach, or with the help of an audio CD or audiotape.

This book will teach using imagery and imagined experiences positively, bringing a greater awareness of your thoughts and feelings and how to manage and direct them advantageously.

Imagined experiences can produce changes in blood pressure, brain waves, and other bodily functions ruled by the autonomic nervous system, which is normally beyond conscious control. Because it makes use of imagery and senses, the impact of guided visualization on both your body and your mind can be considerable.

> GUIDED VISUALIZATION CREATES AN IMAGINARY EXPERIENCE WITH FAR-REACHING RESULTS.

For example, as you experience the first scripted exercise, you will imagine a peaceful place in nature where you will be directed to notice the sights, sounds, scents, and even the taste of this special place. You may reach out and touch a tree or run your hand through the water of a trickling brook.

When you add sensory elements to the images, your subconscious does not recognize the difference between imagination (guided imagery experiences) and reality. The subconscious understands images more clearly than words. Thus, experts consider imagery the dominant "language" of the subconscious.

Imagery also acts as a bridge between the conscious and subconscious. By consciously choosing the images you hold in your mind, you can communicate with your subconscious—the gatekeeper to your deepest motivations and emotional experiences.

The brain has two hemispheres that process thoughts in different ways. With the left hemisphere, we think in terms of words and logic, and with the right hemisphere, in terms of images, sounds, and feelings.

The two hemispheres also process information differently. The left brain processes sequentially (one bit of information at a time), while the right brain processes simultaneously (all information at the same time) and has the ability to grasp the big picture. A right-brain perspective may allow you to develop creative solutions to job-search issues... invaluable in the healing process. Guided visualization engages both left- and right- brain activity.

I am sometimes asked how guided visualization compares to positive thinking. Norman Vincent Peale, author of *The Power of Positive Thinking* (1952, 1996) and *Positive Imaging: The Powerful Way to Change Your Life* (1982), wrote in the latter: "Imaging is positive thinking carried one step further. So powerful is the imaging effect on thought and performance that a long held visualization of an objective or goal can become determinative."

A good illustration of this is how I connected with the publisher of my first book. I had been utilizing a number of visualization techniques to support and focus my strong desire and intention to attract a good publisher. I had also taken action by writing a thorough book proposal, attending appropriate conferences and meetings where I might meet editors and publishers, and sending a few query letters—only to be rejected.

The connection ultimately occurred in a way I'd never imagined. I had been invited to present my study results at a California Psychology Association Annual Conference and had just begun speaking when a large portion of the audience began trickling out of the room. Was it something I'd said? In fact, word had spread that a high profile figure (Dr. Joyce Brothers!) had been rescheduled and was now speaking in the room across from me. A few people stayed, a few moved back and forth between rooms, and I moved through my presentation as if I were speaking personally to each person in the room. At that point I was grateful to have anyone in the room.

When the session was over, a gentleman approached me to introduce himself as the editor-in-chief of a psychology-focused publishing house and to ask if I had ever considered writing a book about The Job-Loss Recovery Program. I kid you not, I had my book proposal in my car and the rest is history!

The point of my story is that visualization has worked for me and it can work for you—in ways that you may never imagine. So stay open to new possibilities.

---

## LEARN TO DIRECT YOUR IMAGINATION TO YOUR ADVANTAGE.

---

Belleruth Naparstek, psychotherapist and author of *Staying Well with Guided Imagery* (1994) introduced three operating principles for guided imagery that provide us with important insights into its power. First, the body does not discriminate between the mind's sensory images and actual reality. Thus, the body's systems may react to "only in the mind" sensory images as if they had manifested in the physical reality. Using all five senses in a guided imagery experience ensures that the subconscious will participate as if the experience were actually occurring in your outer reality. For example, imagine for a moment that you are in your kitchen slicing a lemon into four quarters, feeling the hefty knife in your hand and hearing it thump on the cutting board as you slice through the juicy lemon. Now imagine picking up a lemon quarter and sucking the juice from it. If you salivated, then you've demonstrated that the body responds to mental input as if physically real, and that images create bodily changes. Salivation, ruled by the autonomic nervous system, is normally out of conscious control. You may want to turn to Exercise 3 in appendix B for a more detailed scenario of the lemon imagery exercise.

Naparstek's second operating principle states that we become capable of more swift and intense healing, growth, learning, and change when we are in an altered state—that is, a state of relaxed focus. This is largely because when in a state of relaxation, distractions and mental chatter seem to dissolve, and we have more direct access to our subconscious minds. (Getting these effects mandates beginning each of your program sessions with a relaxation exercise.)

Thirdly, she asserts that guided imagery gives us a greater sense of control and mastery over what is happening to us, which promotes enhancement of both our self-esteem and our performance. I found this to be true in my job-loss study. Once the recorded visualization sessions were completed, participants reported increased feelings of control over their employment situation.

## How Guided Visualization Is Used Today

Jack Canfield and Mark Victor Hansen, co-creators of the wildly successful *Chicken Soup for the Soul* book series, selected stories that epitomize goal achievement and success. From their first self-published book they created a multi-million-dollar enterprise of book spinoffs and related products. Canfield was also featured in "The Secret" film that explains The Universal Law of Attraction. Both Canfield and Hansen have noted how the routine use of visualization techniques—with emotion and all the senses involved—played a great part in their success.

You have probably heard the term "mind-body connection." It refers to how thoughts and feelings can impact the body and vice versa. Psychologists have long known about the reciprocal relationship between the mind and the emotions. In other words, what you think affects how you feel, and how you feel affects what you think.

In addition, the expanding field of psychoneuroimmunology examines how the neurological and immune systems interact, and is providing new clinical evidence of the connection between thoughts and health. Scientists can now measure changes in immune cells and the brain in ways that provide objective proof of the connection between them. In her book *Molecules of Emotion* (1997), brain scientist Candace Pert, Ph.D., writes that visualization can increase the blood flow into a selected part of the body and thereby increase the availability of oxygen and nutrients to carry away toxins and nourish the cells. In a wide range of studies, experts have found guided imagery to significantly impact health.

Use of visualization techniques is also linked to improved performance among athletes. It's widely known that competitive sports have become as much a mental game as a physical one, and, for decades, all Olympic athletes have been practicing visualization techniques to increase confidence and peak performance. Swimmer Michael Phelps, the top Olympic gold medal winner of all time (fourteen as of August 2008), used mental rehearsal while in training, and immediately before his Olympic races. Michael Johnson, Olympic sprinter with five gold medals and two world records, says that the only way to stop negative thoughts from creeping into his mind is to replace them with something else. He likes to visualize the upcoming race, concentrating on the start, the weakest part of his race, and thinking about himself shooting off the blocks like a bullet.

In this book you will learn similar techniques to increase your confidence and improve your interview performance.

In his book *Mental Training for Peak Performance* (1996), Steven Ungerleider, Ph.D., a member of the U.S. Olympic Committee Sports Psychology Registry, recounts the personal experiences of athletes who have used visualization training to aid in achieving their great successes, such as Janet Evans, Olympic distance swimmer who won five medals—four of them gold. According to Ungerleider, "The appeal of guided imagery techniques is that we know they work. Not only does research show that imagery works, but numerous athletes swear by it."

Golf superstar Tiger Woods has repeatedly cited mental toughness as his greatest quality. One of his techniques is to study the location of each of the pins on each green while he is still on the driving range. Then he practices as if he is hitting toward each pin, deciding what kind of shots to hit to every green while still on the range.

Jack Nicklaus, one of the most successful golfers of all time, has said that a full 50 percent of his game is psychological. For decades he has used an elaborate visualization process that he calls "going to the movies." In Chapter 7, you will read more about this mental rehearsal process.

Arnold Schwarzenegger was also a pioneer in using visualization techniques as he worked to shape his body. As a professional body builder, he preceded his workouts with visualizations in which he pictured the results he wanted, such as imagining his biceps as big as mountains.

Michael Jordan, the great Chicago Bulls basketball player and successful business entrepreneur, said he has long used visualization techniques daily to plan every step of upcoming games and ensure smooth-running business activities.

Neurolinguistic programming, known as NLP, uses imagery to reprogram the brain in order to achieve selected goals and outcomes. Richard Bandler and John Grinder formulated NLP after observing and modeling the therapeutic techniques of some of the most successful psychotherapists and hypnotherapists, among them Fritz Perls and Milton Erikson. Motivational guru Tony Robbins popularized NLP as a tool for personal growth and empowerment.

Another well-documented use of imagery is to mentally rehearse a painful or anxiety-filled medical event to minimize its harmful impact on the mind and body. Courage, stamina, and the ability to face the unknown are required when faced with such an ordeal. Mental preparation results in keeping attention and energy focused and has effectively reduced pain and anxiety.

The treatment of severe burn injury, as an example, although very successful in saving lives, is frequently regarded as more stressful and painful than the injury itself. Wound care involves debridement— daily removal of the dead tissue from the wound with forceps and scissors. The process is among the most feared and painful of hospital procedures. Patients often describe the method as feeling like being skinned alive. Painkillers are avoided before the procedure, because patients must walk themselves to and from the locations in the hospitals where this process takes place. Exercise is critical to the healing.

In 1988, in a large study using 149 severely burn-injured, hospitalized adults, Achterberg, Kenner, and Lawlis tested three methods of anxiety and pain control and compared them with a no-treatment control group. The methods: relaxation, combined relaxation and imagery, and combined relaxation, imagery, and biofeedback. (The main purpose of biofeedback is to control body functions, such as heart rate or blood pressure.) Each participant received six sessions of the appropriate method in conjunction with daily wound care.

The imagery plus relaxation combination resulted in less muscle tension and fewer pain medications and sedatives than the other groups. The researchers concluded that during acutely painful states, it's more important to learn mental techniques for dealing with the stressful situations than it is to control body functions.

Now, if mental rehearsal can help reduce pain and anxiety under these frightful conditions, surely it can help you remain calm and focused on a job interview.

## *What Guided Visualization Can Do for You*

So often, well-meaning parents teach their children to suppress or otherwise deny their anger and pain rather than helping them to more effectively manage it. Many people have no idea how to even begin taking charge of anger, other than to pretend they simply don't have it—which can lead to explosive and inappropriate expression.

The ability to manage emotions is now called "emotional intelligence," and certain cutting-edge schools are including it in the curriculum. It's about time. For too long now our cultural norms have implied that more evolved or enlightened humans do not experience the heavier emotions such as anger and hurt.

In reality, the masters have learned to recognize, own/feel intensely, forgive, and release heavy emotions so quickly that it appears as though they do not feel them. In other words, one might say they dive deeply and intensely into the emotion, move through it with understanding and forgiveness, and leap back out again. It's a skill we all can learn.

I have used hundreds of guided visualization techniques for countless purposes in my own life over a period of many years. In upcoming pages, I share some of these techniques as well as other methods to help you resolve your heavy emotions and create the future you want.

## *Make an Ally of Your Subconscious Mind*

Your subconscious mind—where many undesirable emotional experiences get suppressed—can become a helpful ally in your healing process. It is capable of releasing the painful emotions and limiting beliefs that hold you back and replacing them with the positive feelings and new beliefs of your choice that can move you forward.

For example, I once held the belief that life would always be filled with struggle, that I couldn't achieve what I wanted without first struggling for it. In fact, that was often the case—I achieved many successes but not without a struggle. You might think my belief formed as a result of having experienced life as a struggle, but it's actually the other way around. I first acquired the belief, role-modeled unintentionally by my hard-working parents, and then my life experiences developed to conform to the belief.

---
YOUR SUBCONSCIOUS CAN BECOME YOUR ALLY.
---

When I became aware that I could be unconsciously attracting events and circumstances into my life that confirmed my belief in struggle, I used visualization techniques to quickly change the belief to "Anything I desire comes to me with ease." Changing a long-held belief can be as simple as making a conscious choice. At other times, you may work with more complex techniques. In chapter 9, I'll discuss more about beliefs and provide exercises for you to change those that no longer serve you well.

The program described in this book is designed to make an ally of your subconscious, allowing you to make the shifts in thinking and feeling you'll need to land a new job quickly.

Visualization techniques have been used for thousands of years in many cultures and traditions. If you're interested in the history of guided visualization, I especially like Patrick Fanning's *Visualization for Change* (1994) and *Guided Imagery for Self-Healing* (2000) by Martin Rossman, M.D. Both books provide a historical framework and describe many visualization techniques for improving emotional and physical health.

## How Confident Are You Right Now?

Self-confidence is, of course, an important attribute for you to project to prospective employers. Unfortunately, losing your job may have undermined your confidence in yourself and your abilities.

Because this program is so easy to implement, you might tend to minimize its benefits. To help you track your increasing confidence level through the guided visualization program, I created the Level of Confidence Questionnaire. As with the Level of Distress Questionnaire, there are no right or wrong answers. The score is for your use only, to compare with your later score.

The questionnaire follows and will appear again in chapter 8, after you complete the final session. That way, you'll be able to compare scores, seeing how far you've come.

So please take a few minutes to rate the questions with thought and honesty. Do it now.

---

# Level of Confidence Questionnaire

Using the following scale from 1 to 10, insert the number that most closely reflects your confidence in your ability to perform that task.

| 1 | 2 | 3 | 4 | 5 | 6 | 7 | 8 | 9 | 10 |
|---|---|---|---|---|---|---|---|---|----|

*Not Confident*        *Moderately Confident*        *Highly Confident*

I can

\_\_\_\_\_ manage the demands created by my job loss.

\_\_\_\_\_ use my social network to obtain job leads.

\_\_\_\_\_ do what it takes to schedule job interviews.

\_\_\_\_\_ perform successfully in a job interview.

\_\_\_\_\_ manage my emotions while unemployed.

\_\_\_\_\_ see my job loss in a more positive light.

\_\_\_\_\_ learn something from my job-loss experience.

\_\_\_\_\_ concentrate my thoughts and efforts on my job search.

\_\_\_\_\_ **Total your score here.**

This score represents your current level of confidence related to your job loss and is for comparison purposes only.

---

## *The Three Levels of a Guided Visualization Experience*

You may experience your guided visualization program sessions on any or all of three emotional levels, depending on your intention and goals.

Relaxation and stress-relief

Closure and success

Wisdom and purpose

The first level promotes relaxation and stress reduction. Each of your sessions begins with a relaxation exercise designed to facilitate a deeper and more meaningful experience. So, at the very least, if you walk through the program without engaging much feeling, you will still benefit by relaxing and reducing your anxiety.

When you participate in the sessions with focused intention and concentration—believing it can work for you and allowing your feelings to surface—the emotional closure and successful job search you seek can take place quickly. Skepticism is healthy; however, while you are engaged in sessions, leave it aside. You will achieve better results if you fully convince yourself of the program's great benefit to you.

If you also seek new meaning and purpose in your life, you may want to use some of the guided visualization techniques to access an even deeper connection with inner wisdom and creativity and to explore any number of issues in your life. I hope you choose this deeper level, which will uncover a well of inner resources with which you can confidently face a fast-changing, challenging world and reach your greatest potential.

## *The Power Tools of Manifestation*

If I could give you power tools to create the best year you've ever had, would that be of value to you? I call them the "power tools of manifestation," and we all use them to some degree, whether or not we are consciously aware of it. They are

1. Desire

2. Expectation

3. Imagination

Let's take them one at a time.

## 1. Desire

Great achievements begin with *desire*. Ask yourself how many times you have achieved an important goal without really desiring it? If you're ambivalent about reaching selected goals, achieving them may be a struggle—examples are when you feel obliged to do something because of family pressures or when you choose a goal because it's expected of you. How committed would you be without desire? How much effort and talent will you devote to a goal you're not certain you want? And what are the chances of achieving that goal under those circumstances, as opposed to, say, a heartfelt goal?

Imagine how it would feel to be intensely committed to receiving your ideal job offer within a certain time frame? Such a commitment can transform a dream into reality by promoting the behaviors you need to generate that event.

What is your greatest work-related desire right now? Stop a moment to make a note of it in your Journal. Feel it, and allow the feeling to permeate your body. Call upon that feeling of desire often as you experience the Job-Loss Recovery Program.

## 2. Expectation

Ask yourself whether you honestly anticipate success. Scientific studies have shown that if you expect to fail, you probably *will* fail. Conversely, if you believe you will succeed, then your chances of success are greatly improved.

Brian Tracy, popular professional speaker, business authority, and author of *Create Your Own Future: How to Master the 12 Critical Factors of Unlimited Success* (2002), teaches what he calls the mental laws that govern our lives. One of these laws is that your expectations determine your attitude and attitude determines your reality. You get what you expect!

A former client told me a story about his daughter, Barbara, who was earning her undergraduate degree. A final exam was approaching in a challenging class, and Barbara's especially bright roommate, who had previously failed the exam and felt defensive, derided Barbara, saying she would never pass the exam. Barbara reportedly accepted the prediction and thought, "How can I pass if she couldn't?" She began to imagine the consequences of failing and became extremely anxious. She studied many hours for the test, but anxiety interfered with her retention and testing performance, and she failed the exam —just as she'd expected.

Barbara later met with her instructor, who was surprised at the failed exam because Barbara had always been a good student. They reviewed some of the test questions together, and Barbara got every one of them correct.

What had happened? Barbara had compared herself to her roommate, believed a negative prediction, and went into the exam expecting to fail. She allowed the roommate to significantly influence her thinking, her attitude, and, therefore, her chance of success.

Expectation can affect us in other significant ways as well. Participants' expectations have been shown to impact scientific study results. In the introduction to this book, I defined placebo as a test condition that participants incorrectly believe is the effective condition being tested. Now, I will expand upon that definition, showing how the good effects people seemingly got from their placebo treatments were really a result of their expectations.

A placebo is an ineffective and harmless procedure or technique —a pill with no medication in it, in many cases. A *placebo effect* refers to the positive, measurable results study participants actually get based solely on their beliefs and expectations. In other words, the patient's, or study participant's, response stems from *belief* in the procedure or drug rather than from the procedure or drug itself.

Drug studies are classic examples. Participants are randomly assigned to one of two or three groups: one group receives pills containing the actual medicine being investigated, and a second group (the placebo control group) is given placebo pills containing only sugar. Both groups believe they are receiving the effective medicine. When a third group (the control group) is included, it gets no pills at all.

Typically, the first two groups get positive results. If the medicine is found effective, the first group, which received the actual medicine, will get a much larger positive effect. Nevertheless, the placebo control group does receive a measurable benefit. The third group, when included, typically shows no effects, since they received no pills.

The placebo result offers but one conclusion: If you believe you're getting the real thing and expect to benefit, then you will. Scientists don't know why this occurs, but they know that it does.

Thus, the second power tool, expectation, can change the course of your life. It's important to examine whether you honestly expect success or failure in both your job search and this program. Are your expectations your own or have you adopted someone else's? Expectation is such a powerful tool that we want to be sure it's working for us and not against us.

## 3. *Imagination*

I cannot overemphasize that if you want to consciously change, grow, and reach selected goals, your imagination is an indispensable tool. With it you'll explore, rehearse, and integrate the desired event or circumstance.

If you've ever imagined yourself in your future—whether working to meet a deadline or spending a leisurely Sunday afternoon doing something just for yourself—you have experienced a Future Self. This imagination process has been shown in studies to enhance effort, persistence, and performance in working toward goals. Imagining a positive Future Self has also been linked to increased life satisfaction. Internally meeting your Future Self can bring you mental, emotional, and behavioral benefits.

Another rewarding use of imagination is for mental rehearsal. This use has become increasingly popular in the field of athletics, where goal achievement is paramount. Mental rehearsal can increase your sense of effectiveness and competence and can enhance emotional mastery and problem solving. Research also shows that mental rehearsal increases the perception of having control over a stressful situation, such as job loss.

Coupling mental rehearsal with desire will also help you translate thought into action by increasing your expectancy about the imagined event, such as receiving a job offer.

This subject would not be complete without a word about the underlying, critical role of intention. Intention is the use of will. Every thought, feeling, and action is motivated by an intention. Become conscious of your true intentions before choosing a path or goal. Then desire, expectation, and imagination can bring it about. Otherwise, intention can oppose or even sabotage your goal.

## *Fringe Benefits*

When your power tools are plugged in, you may find you get more than you ask for. For instance, I never imagined being profiled in *Fortune Magazine*, or interviewed by *The Washington Post*. My beliefs were too limiting to think a small-town girl like me could be cited in the nation's top business publications. Nevertheless, it happened.

Many people probably thought, "Isn't she lucky?" Do you think Donald Trump is lucky? My guess is that, on some level, he knows about these power tools of manifestation. Don't you think he walked over and over again down that block in New York City where the Trump Tower now stands, passionately imagining what it would look like and how he would make it happen? Don't you think he dreamed about it at night—seeing the construction and hearing the sounds of it being built while mentally walking through the building? You bet he did. We don't all want to be Donald Trumps, of course. But we can create our own luck.

> ## YOU CAN CREATE YOUR OWN LUCK.

In my case, my deepest desire was to make the Job-Loss Recovery Program available to displaced employees everywhere. I imagined thousands of job seekers using it to achieve healing and decrease landing time. And I mentally experienced my Future Self—the person I imagined myself to be in the future— feeling the joy of that achievement.

One day, following my presentation to a business group, a woman approached to tell me how distraught she was. "I have a daughter in Los Angeles who was laid off in a high-tech downsizing. She's been out of work for seven months now and is extremely depressed. I'm at my wit's end and don't know what to do. Do you think you can help her?"

I began working with her daughter, Sarah, an ambitious, single woman in her early thirties. She had held a high-paying job in a software company and was now waitressing to make ends meet. She felt hopeless and hadn't had a good night's sleep in several months. Sarah had never used guided visualization before and approached it with skepticism, but she was in crisis and willing to try anything. She had several phone sessions with me and completed the Job-Loss Recovery Program's visualization recording.

Since the depressed high-tech industry was not hiring, she began seeking work in the music industry—an arena that had appealed to her for many years, but in which she had no experience. Within thirty days, Sarah called me to say, "You won't believe what happened!" She had accepted a position—a foot in the door—with a music company. She stepped into a field she loved with no prior experience—a feat all of her friends had said was impossible. Sarah made her own luck, too.

Now, back to *Fortune Magazine*. While Sarah was still looking for work, a reporter from the magazine called to talk with her about the job market; he was writing an article on job loss. She told him about an effective new visualization program that was helping her and suggested he talk with me. He said he'd love to do that and took my phone number. When the reporter didn't call within a week, I asked Sarah for his e-mail address and composed an introductory e-mail to him. I can tell you I sweated over the composition of that message, but finally I hit "Send" and was ready for action.

Within twenty minutes, his return e-mail popped into my screen. "Let's talk," it said. We set up a phone interview, and he profiled my program in the magazine.

The message I hope you take from this story is that you have to create your own luck and look for opportunities everywhere. Always ask for what you want and then take action to get it—provided, of course, that you harm no one. When your intention is clear, when you have strong desire and an expectation to succeed, and when you use imagination to explore and experience the desired goal, success may come faster than you expected—and in more ways than you imagined.

Thus, desire, expectation, and imagination are powerful tools you can access to help you on your journey to reemployment. There will be ample opportunities to engage each of them in this program.

Now that you've been introduced to guided visualization, let's take a moment to put a sample of it into practice. You may want to read through these instructions first and then close your eyes to experience the scenario with fewer distractions.

Take several deep breaths, inhaling deeply and exhaling fully. Imagine yourself holding your planner and scheduling six guided visualization program sessions. Despite any healthy skepticism, you want to give your best effort to this program in order to receive the most benefit. Sense yourself moving through each of the sessions even though you don't yet know their complete content. Imagine feeling more and more relaxed, letting go of your fears and worries, even enjoying the experiences. Think about how your life is already changing for the better, and how it will feel as you leave the uncomfortable past behind and move forward with new hope and positive expectations. You're taking back control of your life, and it feels good. As you move through the program, sense your confidence growing until you know in both your mind and heart that you are creating the successful future you want and deserve. New directions and exciting opportunities are developing. Belief can be a conscious choice. Make the choice now to believe and to expect that out of crisis and adversity will come success, meaning, and purpose. Now open your eyes and sit with the experience for a moment.

In the next chapter, you'll learn more about the structure of the Job-Loss Recovery Program and how to make the most of it.

# Chapter 3

## *The Job-Loss Recovery Program*

*Don't find fault, find a remedy.*

—Henry Ford

### *The Program's Foundation*

The foundation of this book includes a unique system of guided visualizations that I developed for my scientific study, a system motivated by the knowledge that traumatic losses can block us from moving forward successfully, and a quick recovery is dependent upon emotionally resolving these losses.

The Job-Loss Recovery Program uses a combination of relaxation exercises plus four visualization scenarios that you will undertake repeatedly in just six sessions.

In sessions 1, 2, and 3, you will mentally and emotionally resolve the heavy feelings associated with the loss of your job. If you've been holding on to anything you'd like to say to a former employer, here is where you'll find resolution. I will teach you the method of express yourself in your sessions, which will help bring closure to any of your unresolved feelings. This critical first step of emotional resolution begins the process of leaving the past job behind and moving on to a new one.

---

THE JOB-LOSS RECOVERY PROGRAM GUIDES YOU THROUGH SIX SCRIPTED SESSIONS TO:

- RESOLVE JOB-LOSS DISTRESS
- BUILD YOUR SELF-CONFIDENCE
- IMPROVE INTERVIEW PERFORMANCE
- LAND THE JOB OF YOUR CHOICE

---

In these sessions, I will also mentally introduce you to your happiest, most successful Future Self. This can help you build hope and self-esteem, as well as prompt some great ideas. This simple experience will also increase your motivation and improve your performance in the job search.

In the final three sessions, you will mentally rehearse peak performance job interviews. In addition, you will mentally create and interact with your Mentor, from whom you will feel unconditional support. This experience can help you to further develop your career dreams and access wisdom deep within you.

Overall, the scenario experiences are relaxing and positive. If this is your first exposure to guided visualization, don't worry about not having the skills. I will instruct and guide you through each step and you will improve with practice.

## Visualization Scripts and How to Use Them

The program utilizes guided visualization scripts, which are scenarios or narratives designed to guide you through specific mental experiences. You may also think of the scripts as instructions. The basic program scripts are divided into two modules: Module 1 and Module 2.

In addition to these two basic scripts, I've provided supplemental scripts (most of which appear in appendix B) to enhance your visualization skills and provide you with even more resources to promote reemployment success. These scripts are labeled as numbered exercises to distinguish them from the Module 1 and Module 2 program scripts in the text.

There are different ways to use the scripts. I recommend you listen to a prerecording of them, especially if guided visualization is new to you. Even with my many years of experience, I often prefer to use a prerecording. It frees me to follow along and become deeply immersed in the experience, rather than have to think about what I should do next.

If you choose to record yourself, practice reading the scripts aloud very slowly before you record. Pause where indicated by ". . ." to allow the suggested experience to unfold. Keep a relaxed tone in your voice because you will want to listen to a calm, slow-paced voice while in session. Use your own name as you read, to reinforce the messages.

Your own voice should also sound pleasant to you. If it doesn't, you might ask a family member or friend whose voice you do like to read or record the scripts for you. Consider playing soothing music while recording the Basic Relaxation Skills script. Choose whatever music makes you feel calm and peaceful. An extremely slow rhythm usually accomplishes this best. Check the sound quality early in the recording process by recording a line or two of script and then playing it back. You can then adjust the settings. This trial run can also prevent you from accidentally leaving the pause button on, a frustrating (and surprisingly common) experience after you've recorded for twenty minutes.

If your choice is to read the scripts each time instead of listening to a recording, then read through them a couple of times prior to becoming focused and involved in the experiences. This will give you a clear understanding of the entire flow and will enable you to later keep your eyes closed as you walk through the mental scenarios. If you need prompting while in a deep state of relaxation, you can open your eyes briefly to glance at the script. It's a good idea to highlight key transition points in the script ahead of time, to help you find them quickly.

## Program Structure

Each of the two scripted modules is repeated three times, providing the total of six sessions. Again, repetition adds important impact to the experience and is critical to the program's success. Although you will follow the same basic procedure for three sessions, each one of your applied personal experiences will be unique. For example, as you execute Module 1's process of resolution and closure, you may choose to mentally express your thoughts and feelings to your former boss while in Session 1, and then to mentally express your sense of personal loss to former colleagues in Session 2.

Another example: In sessions 4, 5, and 6 (Module 2), you will mentally rehearse job interviews and then meet with an inner mentor.

With each succeeding session, communications with your mentor will flow more easily. Input and feedback will become clearer. Further, you may decide each time to mentally rehearse interviews for different jobs, with different interviewers questioning you. In other words, you will follow the same basic procedure in the three sessions, but your actual experiences will be different from each other.

All sessions include the basics of relaxation and establishing an emotionally safe place plus two scenarios, organized in the following way:

## Module 1: Sessions 1, 2, and 3 all include:

Basic Relaxation and Safe Place

Emotional Closure

Meeting Your Future Self

## Module 2: Sessions 4, 5, and 6 all include:

Basic Relaxation and Safe Place

Mentally Rehearsing a Job Interview

Meeting Your Mentor

Don't worry about what to do and when. I will guide you through each step of the entire process. The first sessions in Module 1 begin at the end of chapter 4, and you will begin Module 2 after completing chapter 6.

Schedule no more than one session a day. This will allow enough time and space for greatest mental and emotional absorption and integration of the experiences.

To receive maximum benefit from the program, it's essential to implement it as it's laid out. The scripts were designed to be experienced in the order I've presented. For example, it's important that your job-loss grief is mostly resolved and that you feel closure before moving on to Module 2's mental-rehearsal scenario, because grief and stress can block success. If you participate in a job interview while holding these blocking feelings, they will affect your attitude and performance.

I learned a valuable lesson about attitude in my first corporate sales position. When I was in my mid-twenties a pharmaceutical company hired me to promote baby formula and medications to the pediatric health-care community. On my first morning, while loading the trunk of my car with products slated for delivery to a pediatric hospital unit, I dropped a twenty-pound case of formula on my left foot, breaking three bones. After loudly articulating a few choice words, I drove to a hospital where a medic applied a cast from the knee down.

I was embarrassed and felt very angry with myself. I had so wanted to perform well in my new job and make a good impression on the clients. My mood, needless to say, had soured. The baby formula was needed, however, and I'd always tended to see the positive side of a situation, so I decided to make the best of it. I put on the sincerest smile I could muster under the circumstances and made the delivery that very day.

When I hobbled into the pediatric unit pulling behind me a luggage cart filled with formula, you'd never have known it was my first visit. Heads turned, and several nurses—including the head nurse— approached to help. They called me a real trooper for making calls on the day I broke my foot. We were soon chatting like friends.

The entire month went on in a similar way as I met all of my physician and hospital clients. What an icebreaker that broken foot was!

The decision to look for the best in my situation allowed me to take advantage of an opportunity that I might not otherwise have recognized. Rather than seeing myself as disabled in my new job, I squared my shoulders and ventured forward, reframing the situation positively. Had I approached clients while wallowing in self-pity and anger, I'm certain I wouldn't have been welcomed the way I was. For the first time, I consciously acknowledged the power of positive attitude. It was, indeed, a valuable lesson.

If you're having difficulty seeing anything positive in your current situation, you may find this program will help turn that around. Although the entire program can be completed in six sessions, some clients who have had to deal with more severe job-loss trauma or multiple layoffs have benefited from additional work with Module 1.

Jack is a good example. He was employed by a major shipping service corporation for twenty-five years and had relocated several times as his career progressed. The company played a significant role in his life and, as you might imagine, his layoff left him with painful broken ties. He had also experienced several traumatic work-related events during his years with the company and came to me holding strong issues about the insensitive way the corporation had laid him off. Because of the severity of his trauma, Jack reported reaching full emotional closure only after six sessions with Module 1.

Each person is unique. Let your feelings set your pace. In this way, you will achieve the greatest possible benefit from the program.

## *How to Make the Most of Your Guided Visualization Sessions*

Whether you are new to guided visualization technology or have lots of experience, there are several things you can do to enhance your success with the Job-Loss Recovery Program.

Most people relax more completely while lying down rather than sitting up. In a sitting position, your head and neck are typically not supported, so it's more difficult to fully relax. The idea is to get as comfortable and relaxed as possible. If lying down tends to encourage falling asleep, try a semi-lying position where your head can be supported, yet you're sitting up enough to keep awake. Experiment a little during the first couple of sessions.

If you happen to fall asleep during sessions, you may not be getting enough sleep at night. Practicing the relaxation and visualization skills will help you learn to stay awake while in a deep state of relaxation. You might also try keeping your eyes open during sessions, focusing on a set point directly in front of you.

Remove your shoes and wear loose clothing. I sometimes use an eye mask to block out as much light as possible. This makes it easier to turn inward and focus more fully on the guided visualization scenarios.

Find a room where you can have privacy—perhaps your office or a bedroom—and ask family members to respect a quiet time for about twenty minutes while you are "in session."

If your environment is not quiet, you may want to use a fan as white noise or use headphones to block distracting sounds, whether or not you are listening to recorded scripts.

Have your Journal at hand so that you can make notes while remaining in a quiet, reflective state.

## *No Experience Necessary*

If this is your first exposure to guided visualization technology, you needn't be concerned about your lack of experience. Most of the study's participants had no prior experience using visualization techniques, yet 62 percent of those who used guided visualization found jobs within two months. Had the study included the additional sessions and more in-depth information that this book has, perhaps many more would have become reemployed during that time.

Since most of the participants in the study reported they'd had no previous experience with guided visualization, I was curious to know their feelings about their participation in the process. Therefore, after the last session and again two months later, I asked them to write down how they felt about their study experience and to comment on the overall project. Allison's comments are representative of several.

At age forty-one and a single mother, Allison had joined a company as marketing director just two months prior to her layoff. She had sought reemployment for three months before entering the study through an outplacement firm, and she felt understandably distraught. Allison had no prior experience with guided visualization and was skeptical at first, but she thought it was worth a try. Following her last session, Allison wrote, "I felt relaxed and in control . . . safe and hopeful. Also, this study helped to build inner peace and confidence." Within two months, Allison settled comfortably into a new position as art director for a growing young company.

Here's what other participants had to say:

"Glad I went through this. I will try to remember the process and do it on my own in this and future events."

"Had difficulty staying focused, yet felt extremely relaxed and peaceful."

"I feel more confident and actually think this will help make my transition from my old career to a new career. Overall, I have gained confidence that I will find my perfect job."

"I think the greatest help for me has been in demonstrating the value of guided imagery."

"More in control. Greater sense of perspective. Sessions 1-3 can be used to deal with other life issues. Daily use of the session would have great therapeutic value…"

So, even with no prior visualization experience and a very short introduction during the study, participants felt they received value from their sessions. You can, too.

You are now ready to learn the details of Module 1. I'll start by introducing you to the benefits of relaxation and your first guided visualization script.

# PART II

# The Power of Closure:
# Module 1

# Chapter 4

## *Relax and Create a Safe Place*

*The cyclone derives its powers from a calm center. So does a person.*
—Norman Vincent Peale

## *Benefits of Relaxation*

You will begin each guided visualization program session with a relaxation exercise that includes decreasing muscle tension, slowing breathing, and visiting an imaginary safe place. In addition to reducing stress, the exercise helps you reduce bodily and environmental distractions. As a result, your physical comfort is enhanced, making it easier to focus more fully on your mental experience. Many healing traditions employ this critical first step.

Formal relaxation training is most often associated with the "progressive relaxation" introduced by Edmund Jacobson, M.D. (1938). Progressive-relaxation training involves alternately tensing and relaxing sixteen different muscle groups. Recently, researchers have found that progressive relaxation training is equally effective with or without the tensing component; thus, "passive relaxation training" was formally named by James C. Overholser (1990), and is used in this program. In other words, you will relax your muscles without first tensing them.

Relaxation through breathing is a quick and easy way to reduce stress any time, whether at work, paying bills, or running errands. Breathing is affected by your emotional condition. When we feel under stress, for example, we become short of breath. But you can control your breathing by simply becoming conscious of it and slowing it down. By calming your breathing, you'll also calm your body and mind, reducing your stress level.

To give yourself a respite from tension and stress, you'll need to breathe deeply into your diaphragm. When you watch a sleeping baby breathe while lying on its back, you'll notice the belly moving in and out. That's the natural and healthy way to breathe. Most of us have developed the habit of shallow breathing, with expansion and contraction of the chest rather than the belly. As you are guided through this program's relaxation script, consciously slow your breathing while taking deep breaths in and out, exhaling fully, and feeling your belly move in and out.

I will also be guiding you through passive relaxation of your muscle groups, focusing on each muscle group and directing it to relax and release any tension it may hold.

Try a bit of the process now. Sit with your feet on the floor or lie down. Place your attention on your feet. Feel all of the muscles in your feet and toes slowly relax and begin to feel very loose and warm. If you find it difficult to sense your feet and toes relaxing, try tensing them first and then relaxing them. This is progressive muscle relaxation, and tensing first will teach your body to recognize and relax individual muscle groups. When you've relaxed this way a few times, you may no longer have the need to tense before relaxing your muscles.

The program's Basic Relaxation Skills script also includes instructions for you to create an imaginary safe place in nature. Once there, you will drink in its calm and peace. All of your guided visualization scenarios will take place, or at least begin, in this safe place. This pattern will condition your mind to promptly return to the relaxed state each time you revisit. In fact, should you feel the need to destress at any time in the course of your day, you may want to take a mini mental trip to your safe place and feel anxiety melt away.

Since relaxation itself has many benefits and applications in your life, I've included a relaxation script in this chapter. It's similar to the script that appears in Module 1. Begin practicing with it now so you can receive help reducing stress right away and be able to relax more deeply when you get to the Module 1 program script in chapter 6.

## Script: Basic Relaxation Skills

*Find a comfortable position. . . . Gently close your eyes. Begin by focusing on your breathing—inhaling deeply . . . and exhaling fully. . . . Allow your abdomen to expand and contract as you breathe deep into your diaphragm. . . . And again . . . breathing in relaxation . . . and breathing out any tension in your body. . .*

*Inhale . . . exhale . . . relaxing more and more . . . becoming more calm with every breath. . . . Imagine any distracting thoughts drifting away. . . . For the moment, your mind is still . . . feeling calm and relaxed now . . . inhaling deeply . . . and exhaling.*

*Enjoy these few moments in peacefulness. . . . Notice the heaviness as your muscles begin to relax. . . . As I count down from five to one, allow yourself to become more and more relaxed. . . . Imagine all the anxiety flowing out of you as you relax deeper and deeper. . . . Five, four, going deeper, three, two, even deeper, and one. . . . Allow these feelings of tranquility to spread through your body. . . . You may notice a warm, heavy feeling coming over you, a sign of deep relaxation.*

*Now move your attention to your feet. . . . Feel all the muscles in your feet and toes slowly relax and begin to feel very loose and warm. . . . Allow the relaxation to spread into your calves as these muscles begin to feel loose, warm, and heavy. . . . Now release any tension you feel in your knees. . . . Now feel your thigh muscles begin to relax, all the tension releasing down, out of your feet and into the earth. . . . This relaxing, peaceful feeling is a gift you're giving to yourself.*

*Now focus on your hips and abdomen. . . Feel all the muscles loosening and relaxing. . . . Release any tension held there, allowing it to flow down and out of your body. . . . Now your back muscles are loosening, feeling warm. . . . Your neck and shoulders, a favorite place to hold burdens, are loosening and releasing any knots blocking you. . . . Continue to relax as you go deeper and deeper.*

*Move your attention to your arms, your upper and lower arms, and your hands. . . . Let go of any burdens and responsibilities. You can pick them up again later. . . . Sense your hands relaxing and warming as the tension flows out through your fingers. . . . Now focus on your jaw, sensing it becoming loose and relaxed. . . . Now your face is relaxing, feeling warm and heavy . . . all the muscles around your eyes, relaxing . . . all around your head, loosening and relaxing. . . . Feel the muscles releasing their knots, the anxiety and tension flowing down and out.*

*Now, take a few moments to scan through your body, noting any remaining tension. . . . Release it now, and let it flow down and out. . . . Allow yourself to enjoy this relaxation and peacefulness.*

*Relax even deeper . . . . Allow your mind to become calm and peaceful . . . . Remember, you can send thoughts and feelings drifting away . . . . Focus on your feelings of deep, peaceful relaxation.*

*Now go even deeper . . . . Imagine yourself in a very special and safe place where you can be alone and at peace . . . . You can create your safe place and change it any way you like at any time. . . . Maybe it's a secluded place in nature, such as an ocean beach with gentle waves lapping at the shore, or a forest clearing with the comfortable sounds of birds . . . or perhaps a mountain meadow with a soft breeze whispering through the wildflowers . . . any place where you feel comfortable and safe.*

*Look around your safe place . . . . Sense the shapes and colors coming into focus, becoming more and more clear . . . . Notice what time of day it is—perhaps the soft light of morning or the colorful setting sun . . . . Listen to the sounds of nature around you. . . . Notice the fragrance in the air . . . . Feel the earth under your feet, or run your fingers through the water that might be there.*

*Make any changes you like; this is your place. . . . No one can come here without your invitation. . . . You are in control. . . . It feels good. . . . Let any distracting thoughts float away. Now come back to full awareness of the room around you . . . feeling refreshed. . . . Allow your eyes to slowly open . . . . Take a few slow, deep breaths, and enjoy the moment.*

Now you're ready to learn how to master your distressing feelings so they no longer interfere with your success and your interactions with others. In the next chapter, I'll show you how to heal the pain of losing your job. I will review the emotional closure scenario of the Job-Loss Recovery Program and provide you with the four steps leading to emotional mastery.

# Chapter 5

## *Mastering Distressing Emotions*

*Anger as soon as fed is dead—'Tis starving that makes it fat.*
—Emily Dickinson

### *Closure Is Critical*

Logically, you may be able to understand why companies, in the throes of downsizing, restructuring, and merging, lay off employees. Many companies have run into financial hardship and must find ways to survive. Layoffs are generally not personal, having little to do with performance evaluations. You may understand this and may even have stoically thought, "This is just part of life, and the only thing constant in life is change."

Of course that's true. Yet, at the same time, you may hear a nagging voice inside shouting, "But they shouldn't have the right to turn my life upside down like this! How do they get away with doing this to people?"

Job loss can ignite anger toward a past employer or shame and rage over vulnerability. These feelings can lead to a need to blame and punish or to create destructive fantasies directed toward anyone connected to the job's termination. If this has happened to you, these thoughts and feelings very likely conflict with your sense of conscience and lead to guilt or shame over such aggressive impulses.

These feelings are normal, however, and having them doesn't make you a bad person. We are complex human beings, subject to many kinds of emotions. Although you wouldn't seriously consider acting out your destructive fantasies, denying to yourself that you have them will impede your ability to move on. And as you know, suppressed feelings may also leak into your job-search interactions and sabotage your goals.

Imagine you're an interviewer listening to a candidate discuss prior experience with his or her company, and you clearly sense an underlying resentment toward the former employer. Do you want to add this person to your team? Probably not. In fact, many employers say they consider attitude even more important than resume.

I know this is true, based on my former experience as an executive search consultant. Companies hired me to recruit and interview job candidates for available management positions, and I learned to identify individuals who harbored unresolved issues about their former employers. Experience taught me these people weren't first-choice candidates.

For example, when I interviewed Janet, jobless for a month since her layoff, she presented an impressive resume and great references. Janet had most recently worked for five years as a department director with a high-tech company in Orange County. She appeared capable and enthusiastic, and I arranged to have her meet one of my client companies.

Executives from the company interviewed Janet on three separate occasions but finally decided it wouldn't work out. Some probing on my part revealed that she had a chip on her shoulder that was not immediately apparent and, as a result, wouldn't fit well into the company.

When I discussed attitude with Janet, she expressed surprise but seemed to understand. She then told me the story of her layoff. As she was arriving at her office one morning, Janet's supervisor met her at the door. He was flanked by two security guards, and he told her about the beginning of a wave of layoffs that had eliminated her position. Janet was stunned and became even more so when her supervisor requested she gather her personal belongings and leave immediately. The guards escorted Janet out of the building. She hadn't seen it coming and felt disrespected, belittled, and very angry.

> REACH CLOSURE TO AVOID TAKING
> UNWANTED EMOTIONS INTO YOUR JOB
> SEARCH.

In the ensuing weeks, Janet's upsetting feelings continued, and she had no idea how to resolve them. Instead, she did her best to ignore them and move on. It's no wonder Janet's underlying resentment seeped into her interviews.

Another result of emotional suppression is that no one can squelch one emotion without affecting all others. Not allowing yourself to experience grief effectively blocks your ability to feel positive emotions, as well. It then becomes extremely difficult to muster the energy and enthusiasm needed to execute the most effective job search.

Have you ever felt truly depressed? I mean for days or weeks at a time, not just for an hour or two. If so, it may have felt as if you lived in a void, cut off from all emotions except sadness and hopelessness, and removed from the world. You probably couldn't feel anything very deeply—neither anger nor enthusiasm. You likely felt stuck and couldn't seem to get motivated to accomplish anything. Depression is often the result of unexpressed anger.

My point is that you don't do yourself any favors by suppressing painful feelings. Humans are distinguished from the animal kingdom largely by our emotions. We are fundamentally emotional beings, as much as we sometimes like to deny it and as painful as it can be.

How then can you avoid taking oppressive emotions into the job search and job interviews, where they can prevent successful performance? By first reaching the emotional-acceptance stage of the grieving process, bringing closure to any painful feelings. What you intensely feel, you can then release.

## Four Steps to Emotional Mastery

The Emotional Closure script of the guided visualization program will guide you through four steps designed to help heal your grief. By learning to master your emotions, you can make them work for rather than against you.

You can honor your emotional self in a way that will set you free by using this four-step process to emotional closure and healing. You can achieve resolution as you move through the steps of this script, which are to

1. *Recognize* your true feelings.
2. *Acknowledge* and express your true feelings safely.
3. *Forgive* others and/or yourself.
4. *Change* which emerges from the previous three steps. Make new choices for growth and positive possibilities.

## 1. *Recognition*

First, consciously recognize what you truly feel. That seemingly simple step may be difficult if you habitually have turned away from emotion, refusing to acknowledge any uncomfortable feelings. Getting in touch with those feelings may also be a little scary, and that's understandable. After all, no one wants to feel destabilizing stress and pain.

The controlled, conscious way you will be dealing with your feelings in this program, however, ensures that you won't get carried away with emotion. Understand that you may have accumulated many different feelings related to your job loss, now indistinguishable from each other and milling about just below the surface of your consciousness. General anxiety often results. Recognizing your feelings is the first step toward relief.

Take a moment now to identify your various feelings. If you need prompting, look back at the list of job-loss grief symptoms in chapter 1, and at your responses to the Level of Distress Questionnaire. Make a note in your Journal of the different feelings you can identify within yourself.

If you're having difficulty recognizing your specific feelings, go to appendix B and do Exercise 1: Recognizing Your Feelings. Do that now.

## 2. *Acknowledgment*

The second step to bringing closure to these feelings is to acknowledge or own them. *Accept them as your feelings.* This step usually involves expressing them in some safe way, with a preplanned time for your expressing, which will take place shortly in the Module 1 program script. You will imagine expressing your feelings to someone responsible for the loss of your job and will receive a satisfactory response.

Emily Dickinson made an important point with just a few words, which I quoted at the start of this chapter: "Anger as soon as fed is dead. 'Tis starving that makes it fat." In other words, anger dissipates when expressed appropriately. On the other hand, anger is exacerbated when it's unacknowledged or suppressed.

As you think of the moment you were laid off, the feelings that erupted within you at that time may bubble up. Images retain the emotions originally associated with them. In this program, you will reenact the imagery of that moment in what feels like a satisfying way to you, and more empowering feelings will replace the distressing ones. Receiving the response that you wanted can heal a stronghold of painful emotions. Thus, control of the imagery gives you control of your emotions.

For example, assume you think the boss specifically selected you for layoff instead of a certain colleague, despite the colleague's poor job performance compared to yours. In the emotional-resolution scenario of this program, you might imagine telling off the boss (or bosses) and then listening while they apologize, explaining how your absence left a great void because of the high value the department placed on you. Or maybe you can imagine that a superior reamed them for letting you go.

When you immerse yourself in the scenario using all five senses, the subconscious will believe it's occurring in your outer reality and will support all of the steps toward emotional healing. You'll soon see the results.

In your Journal, make a list of all the people related to your job loss to whom you would like to speak your mind. It may include a former supervisor, the company president, colleagues left behind, or any number of others.

## 3. *Forgiveness*

That brings us to the third step, forgiveness. Most of us know that to forgive those who have injured us in any way is the right thing to do. The old adage "Forgive and forget" makes a lot of sense, because unless we do forgive, we cannot truly forget. You may not realize that the forgiver always benefits more than the one being forgiven.

Stanford University professors have done some interesting research on forgiveness. Fred Luskin, who heads up the Stanford Forgiveness Project research, believes forgiveness has great emotional and physical benefit. His studies show that learning to forgive produces healthier people.

Luskin provides three steps for learning the process of forgiveness (Dolbee 2001). The first step is to not rush it. Pushing to forgive before allowing yourself to really experience the hurt feelings thwarts your ability to forgive honestly and sincerely.

Therefore, when I suggest in the Emotional Closure script that you forgive those who have caused you pain, don't do it until you can do it honestly and sincerely. If you forgive by rote, without thought for meaning, you may as well not forgive at all.

> ## WHEN YOU FORGIVE SOMEONE, YOU BENEFIT MORE THAN THE ONE FORGIVEN.

Luskin's second step is to realize that forgiveness is about you, not the offender. In other words, forgive to heal your own life. When you hold a grudge or harbor other negative feelings, you stay emotionally connected to the offender. Forgiving sets you free.

The third step is learning to not dwell on the pain inflicted by others. Look for the beauty and the positives in others and in life. Please do not interpret this to mean you should turn away from—avoid or deny—any emotional pain you honestly feel. Learning how to process painful feelings in order to release them is the objective.

When actively seeking the positive, you'll notice how circumstances that once caused great wounds don't arise nearly as often. And when those situations do arise, you will frequently choose a different response. For example, the next time you have a negative run-in with someone, you may not feel hurt at all, or you may have discovered how to process the hurt and do away with it quickly.

Don't confuse forgiveness with justice. Forgiveness doesn't mean condoning bad or illegal actions. Even after forgiving someone, you can still seek justice, when warranted.

Remember, you may need to forgive yourself as well as others. Anger directed inward sabotages self. It damages both confidence and self-esteem and can therefore negatively affect your job-search performance.

Mike came to me with four months of unemployment behind him. He had a background in sales and service in the high-tech industry, which included twelve years with a major telecommunications company. He'd earned an MBA in executive management and then accepted a better opportunity with another company. But eventually he was caught in a downsizing and laid off. Mike then secured a management position with another telecommunications company. Two years after he joined them, they merged with a corporation that retained their management staff following the merger. Once again, Mike was laid off. When he saw the *Fortune Magazine* article about my career-transition program, he clipped it out, but then forgot about it. Months of unemployment later, it turned up under a stack of papers, and Mike called me.

MAKE NEW CHOICES FOR A NEW FUTURE.

When I spoke with him, Mike was looking for a more stable industry where his skills would be transferable. He alluded to "all the degradation" he had experienced in his job search and told me he felt "battered down." I noticed that Mike didn't speak harshly or resentfully about any of his former employers. On the contrary, he said they did what they had to do. "I don't begrudge them for any of it. And I probably should have seen it coming." He blamed himself for not being prepared and for not beginning a job search before being forced to do so. He also blamed himself for putting his entire 401k portfolio in company stock rather than diversifying it.

Mike reproached himself, just as you may be placing blame on your own actions or reactions to your circumstances. You must process that blame just as surely as if it were directed at someone else.

To accomplish this, imagine yourself as the target in the Module 1 exercise, and express your feelings to yourself as you would to someone else. Follow through, as well, with receiving a satisfactory response and forgiving yourself when you're ready to do so. After all, you probably did what you thought was best at the time. Forgiving yourself is critical to freely and successfully moving on.

Now look at the list of your feelings and the people you want to talk to that you made in the previous section. To this list, add all those you want to forgive, even though you may not feel like you can forgive them at the moment. Include yourself, if applicable.

## 4. *Change*

The fourth step in the process of emotional closure is to change. Once you've recognized your true feelings, acknowledged and safely expressed them, and forgiven yourself or others, you will be ready to make new choices for growth and positive possibilities in your career.

This step often emerges naturally when you've accomplished the previous three. Your choices will come from a place of new perspective—that of a confident self, free of constraining emotions and limited insight. Therefore, you can understand why the choices and decisions made at this point may vary greatly from those made while in the throes of pain.


In the next chapter, you'll learn about a straightforward technique called Meeting Your Future Self that can increase your satisfaction with life. You will then begin Module 1.

# Chapter 6

## *Meeting Your Successful Future Self*

*Dream big dreams! Imagine that you have no limitations, and then decide what's right, before you decide what's possible.*

—Brian Tracy

### *Moving Toward Your Future Self*

Research has shown that envisioning successful Future Selves—or possible selves—increases effort and persistence and improves performance. This simple process has also been linked to an increase in life satisfaction. Internally meeting your possible Future Self can bring mental, emotional, and behavioral benefits.

In other words, you can direct your own growth and development through the mental construction of one or more possible Future Selves. The process begins with your self-image and takes on components that represent what you could become and what you'd like to become in the future.

Let's say you worked in middle management in your last position. You were doing well, had high self-esteem, and set a realistic career goal of becoming vice president. You had a strong desire for the position and could so clearly imagine being in that role with your company that you already felt a sense of satisfaction and accomplishment.

You were, in fact, envisioning your Future Self as vice president, although you may not have been consciously aware of the process. My point is that you can now direct and use this practice to your significant advantage.

When you hold an image of having reached a desired goal, that vision produces a processing of information leaning toward the goal. You begin to feel more in control of your situation, and it then becomes possible to formulate more efficient plans to create it. As a result, the probability of actually creating it increases, especially if you can anticipate and experience the feelings associated with—and have strong desire for—the final result. It's easy to understand why envisioning a successful Future Self is often associated with improved performance.

In three studies, all relating imagery to performance, researchers Ruvolo and Markus (1992) found that people who imagined themselves as future successes outperformed those who imagined themselves as future failures.

In the first study, they specifically examined the effects of guided imagery tasks. They designed three conditions for comparison and randomly assigned the 105 undergraduates who participated.

- Condition 1 imagined having success in the future because of hard work.

- Condition 2 imagined being unsuccessful in the future despite hard work.

- Condition 3 participants were put in a good mood (control group, no imagery).

On a subsequent task involving effort, as well as a task involving persistence, those who imagined being successful clearly performed the best.

The other two studies were variations of the first. In both, participants who imagined being successful in the future outperformed those who imagined being unsuccessful.

In summary, envisioning success promotes the development of plans and strategies necessary for achieving success. In the process, you become more motivated to make it happen and can often overcome any related anxiety, fear, and lack of self-confidence.

By the same token, imagining failure works the same way. For this reason, you certainly don't want to give energy to images of failure. So be sure to monitor your thoughts and take responsibility for your mental images.

We often have multiple ideas and images of who we can become and what we can accomplish in this lifetime. Career transition is an excellent time to explore those ideas to aid in determining where your greatest interests and talents lie and to develop clarity about the direction you want to take. Knowing what you want will allow you to focus your efforts more successfully on your job search. It will also make you a more desirable job candidate. Yogi Bera once said, "If you don't know where you're going, you'll end up someplace else."

Take a moment to do a short, supplemental exercise before meeting your happiest and most successful Future Self in the Module 1 program script. It is Exercise 2 in appendix B, called "Recognizing Future Possibilities." The exercise is designed for you to try out several different images of what your future might look like. In it, you'll imagine two or three possible Future Selves.

If you already feel intensely committed to a particular direction, you may want to skip this exercise. However, it could still provide you with valuable information about yourself.

## Sarah's Progress

Do you remember Sarah, the young woman I introduced in chapter 2? She had been laid off for seven months when she came to me. She'd had no visualization experience and some skepticism about the program. She'd held a high-paying job in the high-tech industry and had taken a job waitressing in a café to pay the bills.

Before you embark on your journey of discovery and healing, I would like to share Sarah's progressive healing experience with Module 1 of the Job-Loss Recovery Program. She wrote about her thoughts and feelings after every session and has given me permission to share her journal.

## Session 1

*Very soon after I began to relax I was able to almost lose feeling in my body as I slipped into my safe place. It took me a while to decide what my safe place would be, but I was able to find one and be happy with my choice. I was able to bring myself back to the day of my dismissal, and I was surprised as to how much I remembered about that day. I remembered all the feelings that I had, and I was able to admit things that I had pushed away. The resentment and disbelief came flooding back. I told my boss how disappointed I was about her inability to be honest with me, how she should have fought for me, or how she should have at least let me fight for my job. I let her know that I thought her behavior was wimpy. I let her apologize, since I know she did feel bad. I told her how bad I felt that she didn't keep in touch with me, and she said it was because she didn't feel right about the experience. I like picturing my future self. She looked a lot like my former self: successful, in control, effective, likeable. She had presence. And I realized that I was still that person. But she was different. She was calmer, knew herself better, and had other things in her life besides a career. She was more open, nurturing, at home in her own body. She was happy and content.*

*When I came out of the reverie I noticed how relaxed I was. I wanted to stay in my safe place a little longer and spend more time with my future self. I liked picturing the future. I felt more calm and forgiving of myself. I felt that it was important to start believing in myself again.*

## Session 2

*This time I fell even deeper into the reverie. Unfortunately, my thoughts drifted a little more than the first time, so I had to gently concentrate on focusing on the visualization exercise. But I also was able to think of different things to say to my boss about her behavior and choices. I'm beginning to feel a lot less resentment and more confident in myself and my talents and skills. I'm realizing that the job loss wasn't my fault and that there was nothing I could do to prevent it. I know I really need to focus on my strengths and not focus on what happened in the past. It's time to move on and believe in myself again, like all the people in my life do. When I pictured my future self this time, I also let my thoughts go, but I'm not even sure where they went. I do know that I can achieve my dreams instead of focusing on how I'm going to pay my rent and how my career has changed. I need to really believe that I can achieve my goals and that I deserve success because I've earned it.*

## Session 3

*This session further cemented my belief in myself. I even felt that my future self was me, now. I believed that I had all the skills and feelings of my future self, that all I needed now was the chance to prove myself. I used to be so self-confident—a feeling that I had because I was excellent at my job—and I need to regain those feelings. I am still the same person that I was, and I'm really starting to believe that. I feel stronger, more capable of pushing myself to realize my dreams.*

You'll hear more from Sarah in chapter 8.

## *Implementing Module 1*

You're now ready to implement Module 1, which is comprised of the first three guided visualization sessions in the Job-Loss Recovery Program. The module includes relaxation plus the following two scripts: Emotional Closure and Meeting Your Future Self. Below, an introduction to each of the scenarios provides a summary and suggestions to make your sessions even more powerful.

The complete script for Module 1 follows the introduction.

Your visualization skills and, therefore, the impact of your sessions will improve with use. If you haven't used guided visualization before, I recommend you practice a few brief exercises before you implement Module 1. These supplemental exercises were designed to sharpen your visualization skills and can be found in appendix B. They're grouped in Exercise 3: Refining Your Guided Visualization Skills. Do them now.

As your guided visualization experiences become more three-dimensional and encompass all five senses, they will become more associated than dissociated. What I mean is that, in the beginning, it will probably seem as if you're watching yourself move through the scenarios on your mind's internal screen. In other words, you'll be more dissociated from the action. In this state, the images are typically vague and unclear. Later, as you become intimately involved by using your senses and emotions in the scenarios, you'll feel more associated, as if they're actually happening to you now, rather than to someone you're watching.

At times, you will want to use both states. For example, in the emotional-closure scenario of your first session, you'll begin from a dissociated perspective and then shift into an associated perspective. First, you'll see yourself through a window in your safe place—a dissociated experience. Then you'll imagine moving through the window and into the scene, directly acting out the scene as it happens to you—an associated experience. As your sessions become more associated, they become powerful tools for transformation.

# Evaluating the Impact

The statements listed below refer to your experiences of program sessions. Using the following scale, from 1 to 7, where 1 equals "I do not agree at all" and 7 equals "I agree extremely," place the corresponding number to the left of each of the following statements.

1          2          3          4          5          6          7

*I do not agree at all*                                        *I agree extremely*

_____     Overall, in my session(s), I felt my emotions deeply.

_____     Overall, the images in my session(s) were vivid and specific.

_____     My focus and involvement in the session(s) were very deep.

_____     I have experienced deep relaxation in my session(s).

_____     My sessions(s) were highly meaningful to me.

_____     **Total your score here**

The total score amount is to be used for comparison only. You want to see an upward trend in subsequent scores over the course of the program. As your scores increase, expect the positive impact of the program experiences to increase as well.

## *Module 1 Script Introduction*

The first half of the program—Module 1—includes two key experiences, summarized below. Remember that all of your sessions will begin with the Basic Relaxation Skills script.

### *Emotional Closure*

To begin Module 1, you will breathe deeply and slowly, relax your muscles, and go to your safe place. There you will see a large, one-way window. You can see yourself through the window at your former job, perhaps when you first felt something was wrong or when you were told you would be laid off. It's your choice. Feel yourself being gently drawn through the window into the scene. There, you can express your thoughts and feelings safely, restoring justice and balance without fear of retaliation. You will also receive a response that is satisfactory to you and have the opportunity to forgive yourself or someone else —when you're ready.

When executing your sessions, adapt selected segments of the script to your specific situation. For example, when the script refers to speaking your mind to a former boss, you may want to make it the company president, a former colleague, or even yourself.

## Meeting Your Future Self

You will then meet and interact with the most ideal, successful, wise, and loving self you can now imagine becoming in this lifetime. It may be one you met in the exercise, or it may be one you haven't yet imagined or thought possible. Using your imagination in this way stretches your limits of what you can conceive as possible. You will also receive a gift from your Future Self. It may be tangible or not—an object, a symbol, a word or thought. The gift can open possibilities to advance you on your path to becoming more of this Future Self.

### Alternate Program Structure

The Job-Loss Recovery Program is organized in the exact structure that was used in my job-loss study. The structure's proven success warranted no change.

When I initially created the study protocol, I knew the program had to be compact, as well as quick and easy to implement. Otherwise, displaced employees would never agree to complete it, and I would have no study participants. So I combined the program scenarios to make two modules to achieve the program's goals with fewer sessions than by stringing out the scenarios in single sessions. For example, Emotional Closure and Meeting Your Future Self are experienced in one session as Module 1, rather than as individual sessions. I then instructed participants to repeat each of the two modules three times, the minimum amount of repetitions to yield success based on my experience and education.

However, since you're not a study participant, you may prefer to take a little more time to complete the program than they did. I've developed an alternate program structure you may follow if that is your preference. In that case, each of your sessions would include one fewer experience and, as a result, it would take twelve sessions rather than six to complete the program.

To help you make the better choice for you, I'll list some considerations for each. Let's call the original structure Choice A, and the alternate structure Choice B.

## *Choice A*

- The program can be completed quickly, in six days.

- The structure proved successful in the study.

- In Module 1, being with your wisest and happiest Future Self immediately after expressing your most uncomfortable feelings in the Emotional Closure scenario can be extremely uplifting.

- In Module 2, interacting with your Mentor immediately after rehearsing job interviews may supply feedback and insights to improve your next interview rehearsal.

## *Choice B*

- Sessions are shorter, which is important if you find it difficult to put aside twenty minutes at a time.

- If you choose not to record the scripts for playback, sessions with fewer scenarios may be simpler to remember and implement.

With Choice B, the first session begins with the Basic Relaxation Skills plus Emotional Closure scripts. The second session includes the Basic Relaxation Skills plus Future Self scripts. Sessions 3 and 4 and sessions 5 and 6 are repeats of sessions 1 and 2, in that order. Repetition is still important to success. Scripts for relaxation and each scenario appear individually in appendix A, for convenience.

Sessions for Choice B will be organized in the following way:

**Sessions 1, 3, and 5**

- Basic Relaxation and Safe Place
- Emotional Closure

**Sessions 2, 4, and 6**

- Basic Relaxation and Safe Place
- Meeting Your Future Self

**Sessions 7, 9, and 11**

- Basic Relaxation and Safe Place
- Mentally Rehearsing a Job Interview

**Sessions 8, 10, and 12**

- Basic Relaxation and Safe Place
- Meeting Your Mentor

To sum up, you may want to go with Choice A—beginning now with the following Module 1 script—if you prefer a proven program structure and if speed of completion is critical to you. Select Choice B—using scripts in the book's appendix—if you prefer to focus on only one experience per session and if you are willing to take six additional days to complete the program.

## Module 1 Script: Relaxation, Emotional Closure, Meeting Your Future Self

*Find a comfortable position. . . . Gently close your eyes. Begin by focusing on your breathing—inhaling deeply and exhaling fully. . . Allow your abdomen to expand and contract as you breathe deep into your diaphragm. . . . And again . . . breathing in relaxation . . . and breathing out any tension in your body. . . . Inhale . . . exhale . . . relaxing more and more . . . becoming more calm with every breath. . . . Imagine any distracting thoughts drifting away. . . . For the moment, your mind is still . . . feeling calm and relaxed now . . . inhaling deeply . . . and exhaling.*

*Enjoy these few moments in peacefulness. . . . Notice the heaviness as your muscles begin to relax. . . . As I count down from five to one, allow yourself to become more and more relaxed. . . . Imagine all the anxiety flowing out of you as you relax deeper and deeper. . . . Five, four, going deeper, three, two, even deeper, and one. . . . Allow these feelings of tranquility to spread through your body. . . . You may notice a warm, heavy feeling coming over you, a sign of deep relaxation.*

*Move your attention to your feet. . . . Feel all the muscles in your feet and toes slowly relax, and begin to feel very loose and warm. . . . Allow the relaxation to spread into your calves as these muscles begin to feel loose, warm, and heavy. . . . Now release any tension you feel in your knees. . . . Now your thigh muscles begin to relax, all the tension releasing down, out of your feet, and into the earth. . . . This relaxing, peaceful feeling is a gift you're giving to yourself.*

*Now focus on your hips and abdomen. . . . Feel all the muscles loosening and relaxing. . . . Release any tension held there, allowing it to flow down and out of your body. . . . Now your back muscles are loosening, feeling warm. . . . Your neck and shoulders, a favorite place to hold burdens, are loosening and releasing any knots blocking you. . . . Continue to relax as you go deeper and deeper.*

*Move your attention to your arms, your upper and lower arms, and your hands. . . . Let go of any burdens and responsibilities. You can pick them up again later. . . . Sense your hands relaxing and warming as the tension flows out through your fingers. . . . Your jaw is now becoming loose and relaxed. . . . Your face is relaxing, feeling warm and heavy . . . all the muscles around your eyes, relaxing . . . all around your head, loosening and relaxing. . . . Feel the muscles releasing their knots, the anxiety and tension flowing down and out.*

*Take a few moments to scan through your body, noticing any remaining tension. . . . Release it now, letting it flow down and out. . . . Allow yourself to enjoy this relaxation and peacefulness.*

*Go even deeper into your inner world. . . . Imagine yourself in a very special and safe place where you can be alone and at peace. . . . You can create your safe place and change it any way you like at any time. . . . Maybe it's a secluded place in nature, such as an ocean beach with gentle waves lapping at the shore, or a forest clearing with the comforting sounds of birds . . . or perhaps a mountain meadow with a soft breeze whispering through the wildflowers . . . any place where you feel comfortable and safe.*

*Look around your safe place. . . . Sense the shapes and colors coming into focus, becoming more and more clear. . . . Notice what time of day it is—perhaps the soft light of morning or the colorful setting sun . . . Listen to the sounds of nature around you. . . . Notice the fragrance in the air. . . . Feel the earth under your feet, or run your fingers through the water that might be there.*

*Make any changes you like; this is your place. . . . No one can come here without your invitation. . . . You are in control. . . . It feels good. . . . Let any distracting thoughts float away, as you go even deeper.*

*Now, out of the corner of your mental eye, something captures your attention, and you turn to see a large free-standing window somewhere in your safe place. . . . Curious, you move toward it and somehow know this is a one-way window into your world. . . . You can see through it to the other side, but no one can see you. . . . As you look through the window, a scene begins to come into focus. . . . You realize this is you at your former job . . . perhaps when you were told you would be let go. . . . You choose the scene.*

*Now feel yourself being gently drawn through the window and sense yourself there. . . . It may seem like a long time ago, or like yesterday. . . . Look around. . . . Listen to the sounds, perhaps of people talking or of computers or other equipment operating. . . . Mentally reach out and touch something in your environment. . . . Perhaps you slide your fingers across a desk. . . . How did you feel at the time? . . . Others, when laid off, have often felt shock at first, then anger or sadness, anxiety, fear, guilt, or even embarrassment. . . . How did you respond? What actions did you take? . . . Or did you do nothing? . . . Are you angry or resentful? . . . If you are, is it toward others? Or perhaps you're mad at yourself for being vulnerable and losing control of your career.*

*Now invite into your scene, if they're not already there, anyone to whom you want to express your thoughts and feelings without fear of retaliation. . . . Sense them with you, and greet them in your own way. . . . Notice their expressions, their clothing. . . . Remember how you felt, how you feel now. . . . Now set your intention on mentally saying anything you want to say but with no actual intent to harm anyone in reality. . . . As a symbol of your intention to harm no one, sense a protective shield or bubble around you and the other person or persons in your scene.*

*Mentally say what is on your mind. . . . Don't think about choosing your words carefully. . . . Simply express your feelings. . . . If you feel angry, abandoned, or betrayed, tell them about it as they listen intently to you. . . . If you have mixed feelings, express the ambivalence as well . . . perhaps the sadness of losing contact with friends . . . along with anticipation of new opportunities. . . . You may be surprised at some of the feelings that surface within you. . . . Anything you feel is okay. . . . Simply say anything you want. . . . Let it all go. . . . Reach deep within you and release it all. . . . It feels good to release what you have been holding onto. . . . You may feel a sense of relief.*

*Now, how would you prefer to have this person or these people respond to you? . . . Remember, you are writing the script. . . . Listen as they respond in exactly that way. . . . How does that feel? . . . Don't label it, simply feel it, allowing the feeling to wash over and through you.*

*Now, if you like, impose upon them whatever retribution you feel is fair and just. . . . It's entirely your choice. . . . Now is your chance. . . . Perhaps you want them to get on their knees and beg your forgiveness. . . . Go for it. You are in control . . . and you're not intending harm to anyone in reality. . . . They do not resist or retaliate in any way. . . . If they sincerely apologize, accept it or not, as you like. . . . Forgive if you can do so honestly . . . only when you're ready.*

*Think of your safe place now, and find yourself there once again . . . perhaps with expanded perspective. . . . Maybe you discovered anger you hadn't realized was there. . . . Perhaps you surprised yourself by forgiving and feel a weight lifting off you. . . . You are learning more about who you are. . . . You know, too, that you are doing your best, and that new opportunities for work and growth are not limited. . . . If one passes, another will reveal itself. . . . You know that challenges are a part of life's journey and that you have the skills to successfully move through and beyond them.*

*Now, out of the corner of your mental eye, you notice someone standing in shadow at the edge of your safe place. . . . Curious, you move closer. . . . This person looks amazingly like you, yet somehow different. . . . You realize now that this is you at some point in your future. . . . This Future Self represents the epitome of your potential self—the most wise, the most loving, the most happy and successful self you can become in this lifetime.*

*Invite your Future Self into your safe place . . . and as the figure slowly approaches . . . coming more into focus. . . . Look for details. . . . You may or may not see the image clearly—it doesn't matter. . . . Simply sense the essence and existence of this future you. . . . Sense the connection between you. . . . Greet one another in whatever way feels right for you, perhaps a touch or an embrace.*

*And now look into the eyes of this Future Self, and feel the warmth and loving support coming from one who truly knows you. . . . See your current life through the perspective of those wise, loving eyes. . . . Perhaps you're given a sense of what you are truly capable of doing with your abilities in this lifetime. . . . Allow any feelings and images to wash over you. . . . Communicate with your Future Self now, either through words or in images or in a bodily sensing, in any way that feels right. . . . Perhaps you ask for insight into your progress with healing the emotional pain . . . or simply experience being in one another's presence. . . . Take the next minute to do that.*

*Know that you will overcome your current challenges and will be stronger and wiser for it. . . . Forgive yourself, as well as others, for past failures or disappointments. . . . Now imagine having received an offer for the position of your choice. . . . Feel the pleasure of having successfully completed your search . . . and imagine yourself celebrating with your loved ones.*

*Mentally feel the gentle squeeze of a hand on your arm as your Future Self reaches out to you with a gift. . . . It may be an object, a symbol, a word, or a thought . . . tangible or not. . . . Allow it be whatever it is. . . . If it feels right to do so, simply accept it. . . . If you don't understand it, that's all right. . . . For now, it's enough to know that it comes with love.*

*In a moment, you will come back to full awareness of the room where your journey began, feeling relaxed and refreshed. . . . The count from five to one will help you return. . . . Five . . . beginning to return . . . four . . . sensing the feelings in your body . . . three . . . sensing the environment around you . . . two . . . beginning to move around . . . and one. When you are ready, open your eyes and return, feeling awake and refreshed. . . . Take a few slow, deep breaths, stretch if you like, and enjoy the moment.*

## After Completing Module 1

After you've completed three sessions of Module 1 (or six sessions if you selected the twelve-session structure of Choice B), please again complete the Level of Distress Questionnaire. Compare your scores with those you obtained before beginning the program. You should feel closure on the job-related issues that formerly disturbed you, and your stress level should have significantly decreased. Understand that closure isn't "all or nothing" at this point. You may feel resolved overall, yet distress may pop through, from time to time, for a while. Expect continued improvement through Module 2.

If you'd like the satisfaction of tracking the development of your visualization skills throughout the program, the Level of Distress Questionnaire should be followed by the Evaluating the Impact scale. Rate yourself after the first program session, again at the midpoint, and once again after the last session. Keep track of your scores. Feel free to complete it after every program session if you like. You may want to make copies of the scale for that purpose.

I have found that the five statement ratings typically move up together. As you relax more deeply, for instance, your focus will also deepen, permitting you to become more involved in the sessions' scenarios. The experiences, in turn, will become more meaningful to you.

If you have an off day, when the impact scores are a little lower than before, don't worry about it. Remember, you're looking for an improving trend over the course of the program.

# Level of Distress Questionnaire

The statements listed below refer to your inner feelings in regard to your job loss. Using the following scale from 1 to 10, insert the number that most closely reflects your current feelings and state of mind.

| 1 | 2 | 3 | 4 | 5 | 6 | 7 | 8 | 9 | 10 |
|---|---|---|---|---|---|---|---|---|----|
| *Never* | | *Sometimes* | | | *Frequently* | | *Most of the Time* | | |

_____ I have trouble focusing on what I am doing.

_____ I feel anxious.

_____ I feel frustrated.

_____ I have waves of distressing feelings.

_____ I am reminded of my job loss often.

_____ I try to ignore my feelings about my job loss.

_____ I feel depressed.

_____ I have trouble staying motivated.

_____ I feel angry and/or resentful.

_____ I have trouble sleeping because I keep thinking about my job loss.

_____ I feel fearful.

_____ Any reminder brings back stressful feelings.

_____ I have troubling dreams about my job loss.

For this final statement, use a 1 to 10 scale but, this time, 1 indicates *Strongly Disagree* and 10 means *Strongly Agree*. Insert the number that most closely reflects your current belief, as is relevant to your job loss.

_____ Little can be done to change my job-related problems.

_____ Total your score here.

This score represents your current level of distress about your job loss and is for comparison purposes only.

# Evaluating the Impact

The statements listed below refer to your program-session experiences. Using the following scale, from 1 to 7, with "I agree not at all" being 1 to "I agree extremely" being 7, place the corresponding number to the left of each of the following statements.

| 1 | 2 | 3 | 4 | 5 | 6 | 7 |
|---|---|---|---|---|---|---|

*I do not agree at all*                                     *I agree extremely*

_____ Overall, in my session(s), I felt my emotions deeply.

_____ Overall, the images in my session(s) were vivid and specific.

_____ My focus and involvement in the session(s) were very deep.

_____ My experience of relaxation in my session(s) has been deep.

_____ My sessions(s) were highly meaningful to me.

_____ **Total your score here.**

The total score amount is to be used for comparison only. You want to see an upward trend in subsequent scores over the course of the program. As your scores increase, expect the positive impact of the program experiences to increase as well.

---

You may continue to benefit by repeating Module 1 beyond the three times suggested in the program, as Mike did in the last chapter. Because he had several unresolved issues dating back many years with his last company, he worked with Module 1 for six sessions before feeling significant closure on his past.

If you continue to feel frequent distress or depression and don't yet feel resolved—even after further work with Module 1—consider therapeutic counseling as an additional resource.

Did you reach the point in the last guided visualization session where you could honestly forgive everyone involved in your job loss? If not, ask yourself the following questions:

- Was it difficult to get emotionally involved in the visualization scenarios?

- Was my entire perspective dissociated rather than associated?

If the answer is yes to either of these questions, practice the suggested Exercise 3: Refining Your Visualization Skills in appendix B, and execute Module 1 again. If you haven't yet become emotionally engaged in the program, ask yourself why you might be resisting. Answer as honestly as you can.

You've now completed Module 1 of the Job-Loss Recovery Program and are ready for Module 2. In chapter 7 you will learn how mental rehearsal has helped many others and how it can help you.

# PART III

# Getting the Job You Really Want:
# Module 2

# Chapter 7

## *Rehearsing Your Success*

*Before everything else, getting ready is the secret of success.*
—Henry Ford

### *Improving Self-Confidence and Competence*

As you learned in chapter 2, mental rehearsal has burgeoned in popularity and is used in a number of areas of life. Amateur and professional sports enthusiasts alike rely on visualization exercises to prepare for their sports events. To inspire you to use mental rehearsal to ensure winning job interviews and other job-search activities, I'll offer even more evidence.

I briefly noted Jack Nicklaus's approach in chapter 2. According to Nicklaus (1998), before every shot he sees a color movie in his head. First, he sees the ball where he wants it to finish. Then the scene changes and he envisions the ball going there—its path, trajectory, and behavior on landing. Finally, he sees himself making the kind of swing that will turn the first two images into reality.

Kenneth Baum, a leading sports performance consultant and author of *The Mental Edge* (1999), relates that he occasionally encounters skepticism from athletes regarding the power of visualization. "But once they're aware of the impressive body of research into the mind-body connection, their hesitancy comes to a screeching halt that burns the rubber on the soles of their workout shoes".

Coach and former gymnastics champion Terry Orlick, Ph.D., in his book, *In Pursuit of Excellence* (1990), tells how a member of the national archery team used visualization to prepare for international competition.

A former world champion spoke of how, through visualization, she was able to transport herself to the world championship from her practice site. Instead of seeing the single target that was actually in front of her, she saw targets stretched across the field. She was fully aware of her competitors. On her right was the leading Polish archer;

on her left, a German. She could see them, hear them, and feel them. She shot her rounds under these conditions in the same sequence as she would shoot in the real competition. She prepared herself for the competition and distractions by creating the world championships in visualization and by actually shooting under mentally simulated world championship conditions (75).

Mental rehearsal not only improves one's confidence and self-image, it also increases the perception of having control over a stressful situation. When we feel confident and in control, we're able to approach problems with greater clarity and insight, making it possible to manage our actions and any uncomfortable emotions more successfully.

In this scenario of the Job-Loss Recovery Program, you will mentally rehearse job interviews. I have chosen competitive sports as a basis for comparison because both successful sports achievement and successful interview achievement require the same key elements. For example, they are both competitive activities that demand constant focus and concentration. One must have a clear strategy yet be able to think and adapt quickly to changing circumstances.

Visualizing a successful interview performance will prepare you for the competitive environment and potential distractions of the interview situation. You will, of course, include interviewers in your visualization to make it as real as possible. As a result, when you do face a real interviewer, you'll appear as a polished, self-confident professional with a winning attitude.

---

> ## WHEN YOU ARE CONFIDENT AND IN CONTROL, YOU CAN DEAL EFFECTIVELY WITH UNEXPECTED CIRCUMSTANCES.

---

I use mental rehearsal to prepare for a variety of circumstances. For instance, I recently spoke at the kickoff meeting of a businesswomen's organization. Once I had my presentation prepared, I practiced it using both oral and mental rehearsal. I imagined all the details, from being introduced and walking to the front of the room with a smile, to delivering an inspiring message and bonding with a receptive audience, to humbly accepting applause at the end—with the audience standing for me (of course).

But I was in for a surprise. When I arrived at the country-club location, the dinner meeting had been moved outside to the lawn, adjacent to the tennis courts. Registrations had far exceeded expectations, and there just wasn't room for everyone inside. By the time dinner ended and I was introduced, dusk was fast approaching and the tennis courts were lit. The audience faced the courts, located directly behind me. I couldn't imagine an arrangement more distracting for them, as well as for me.

Because I was well-prepared, I delivered my presentation as planned —and also took advantage of several opportunities to add humorous comments: when an insect flew into my eye and when the players shouted scores from the tennis courts. Even though the audience undoubtedly found it difficult to make a strong connection with me under those conditions, I kept going. Had I not kept my composure and a positive attitude, the presentation could have ended in disaster. Needless to say, I didn't get the standing ovation I'd visualized, but I did a good job in a challenging situation.

Although I was unable to control external circumstances, I could control myself. Even after doing my best to mentally rehearse the event, it didn't happen exactly as I'd imagined it. But since I had done the groundwork, I felt confident in my ability to deal effectively with unexpected circumstances. In other words, I had a strong sense of self-efficacy.

*Self-efficacy* is the judgment that you have the capability to carry out the necessary actions to achieve selected goals or performances. It's not about skills but, rather, about the judgment of what you can do with the skills you have.

Low self-efficacy is often accompanied by fear, because the perceived inability to cope with harmful events makes them frightening. When you believe you can effectively deal with a potentially harmful event, such as job loss, you have no reason to fear it. As a result, life experiences or mental exercises that increase your belief in your abilities—your self-efficacy—shrink your fear as well.

For instance, when you successfully perform challenging skills in your mind while feeling positive emotions, your self-efficacy often improves—along with the determination to experience these emotions again in real situations. Anxiety and fear are often reduced as well (Smith 1990).

In *Who Moved My Cheese?* (1998), Spencer Johnson, M.D., tells a story about change that takes place in a maze where four little characters search for "cheese," which acts as a metaphor for anything we want in life, such as a job, money, a relationship, or whatever. One of the characters learned some important lessons as he searched for cheese, one of which was: "Imagining myself enjoying new cheese even before I find it, leads me to it".

In the mental-rehearsal scenario of this program, you will picture yourself, in great detail, achieving and enjoying the position of your choice. The more clearly you can imagine yourself doing that, the more real and believable it will become.

The participants in my guided visualization job-loss study especially liked the interview-rehearsal component. Here are some comments made immediately after the study.

"Currently feeling well prepared for future interviews. Expecting marked improvement on previous weak points."

"I enjoyed them [the sessions]. Feel confident in my ability to have successful interviews."

"Session 6: Was anticipating it being my last session and wanted to fully focus and experience the emotion, calm, and imagery of 'encounters.' Session was very pleasant and heartening."

"Great relaxation. Helps me relax during interviews. Able to visualize myself, and that helps project a better image during interviews."

"I felt confidence and, at times, even though I would have to rewind to correct or think about a convincing statement, I felt the interview was going perfectly."

"I like the idea. I will use it on my own—to play, pause, edit, my own interview movie without the time constraints."

"I liked this process. I felt a lot of positive energy in visualizing a successful interview."

"Very relaxing. In sessions 4 and 5, it was difficult to stay with the imaging of an interview, but by session 6, I was very focused, due to it being just before an anticipated interview for a consulting job."

In chapter 8, I show you how to gain new insights into your career and life to increase your confidence even more. You'll be provided with the Module 2 script of the Job-Loss Recovery Program, which includes mentally rehearsing job interviews. You will then implement Module 2.

# Chapter 8

## *Meeting Your Mentor*

*If you are distressed by anything external, the pain is not due to the thing itself, but to your estimate of it; and this you have the power to revoke at any moment.*

—Marcus Aurelius

### *Access Your Inner Wisdom*

You are now ready to meet your inner Mentor, the final scenario in the Job-Loss Recovery Program. A mentor is part collaborator, part personal consultant, part cheerleader, and part sounding board. A mentor can help you take more responsibility for your own growth and development and can help you come to grips with huge changes— such as career transition. A mentor can also help you increase your self-confidence and motivation.

This inner Mentor can meet your special needs. For example, some people need a great deal of positive feedback, others need challenge; some need someone to hold them accountable, and still others simply need a sounding board.

Who or what is this inner Mentor, really? The concept comes from both eastern and western traditions, dating back thousands of years. It's been referred to by many names, such as the subconscious, inner wisdom, guardian angel, and inner guide. I like to call it the "Inner Mentor." Whatever you choose to call this guidance, you can access it if you honestly seek the truth within yourself. I have been amazed at the insight and understanding that comes from this source—in my clients and in myself.

### *Develop New Insight through Reframing*

Your inner Mentor can help reframe and reappraise events and circumstances in your life. Reframing refers to redefining or reevaluating a situation from a different perspective—usually a more positive one that wasn't noticed before. In chapter 3 I told you my "broken-foot" story. Well, if I had viewed the situation as a tragedy, I might have wallowed in self-pity and thought the worst: "I won't be able to do the job, and my boss will fire me." That's considered a negative frame. Rather than wallow, I decided to make the best of the situation and get on with my obligation. As it turned out, the cast was a conversation starter that gave me an opening to build rapport with my new clients.

Reframing often leads to helpful new insights as well as to a more positive attitude. This is important, since job loss can negatively impact your view of yourself, as well as your view of the world. As you've advanced through this guided visualization program, you've had the opportunity to utilize the language and processes in the scripts to help you reframe the loss more positively and gain new insights about yourself and your circumstances. And as you develop optimistic perspectives, your confidence and motivation will increase.

Richard, the accountant from chapter 1, erroneously felt he deserved to lose his job, thinking it was his fault. His thoughts raced from "What if no employer wants me?" to "I could lose everything." He made a negative appraisal of his situation and, therefore, became anxious and depressed.

Reappraisal, as I mentioned in chapter 1, is the reevaluation of why and to what degree a situation is stressful. It's important to reexamine your initial appraisal of the job loss because you may find that a negative appraisal is the root cause of much of your stress. Understanding the underlying causes for feeling stress is the first step to disarming those causes.

When he reappraised his situation, Richard realized his greatest stress stemmed from his fear of financial ruin. He also learned to reframe his situation as a challenge and began to see that he already had valuable resources to support him through his transition, such as strong business skills and experience. Also among these resources that had been there all along was that his wife earned an income that could support them.

Richard also began to seriously consider starting a financial consulting practice, something he'd always wanted to do. His family supported his dream, once they recovered from the initial shock of his job loss. As a result, Richard felt free to choose new goals and strategies that reflected more of who he really was and wanted to become. In other words, as Richard reframed his situation more positively and reappraised his resources, his depression lifted.

Reframing can also occur when you receive new information.

> # REFRAMING JOB LOSS AS A CHALLENGE CAN AWAKEN NEW OPPORTUNITIES.

Let's say you just returned from a preliminary interview for a position that appeals to you. The responsibilities fit well with your experience, the compensation package is good, and there appear to be sufficient challenges and opportunities for advancement. However, you don't really like the manager you'd be reporting to and, as a result, seriously consider not pursuing the position. Then you run into each other at the tennis club and you realize you have a shared interest. Maybe the manager's not so bad after all. The job opportunity starts looking more desirable. Based on this new information, you have reframed it.

Now that you're aware of the benefits of reframing and reappraising circumstances, you'll want to examine all the frames and appraisals you initially made around your job loss. This is one arena where your Mentor can help.

Your imagination can act as an effective substitute for real life. Your Mentor can provide a tremendous resource and force for your positive growth, if you are open to this concept.

Before you actually meet your Mentor, however, you will first rehearse a job interview. Your Mentor can then provide feedback on the interview as well as suggestions for improvement. But before we go on, let's revisit Sarah's journal to give you a sense of how one person experienced Module 2.

## *Sarah's Progress*

Here are Sarah's impressions of Sessions 4, 5, and 6.

## Session 4

*Due to the helpful nature of Module 1, I was overjoyed to visualize an interview that had me performing without my previous defensiveness and lack of self-confidence. I was able to speak with a positive attitude and without offering any veiled apologies or excuses for my layoff and former inability to find another position. Even though my layoff wasn't my fault, I think I still behaved as if I had to explain it somehow, which came off as defensive and resentful. I just don't feel that way anymore. I think a company would be lucky to have me working for them and representing them. I was able to focus on my achievements and communicate them articulately and with confidence.*

*The mentor aspect was helpful for confidence reinforcement. I think I'll visualize this person even outside of the sessions whenever I need encouragement and a reminder of my talent and skills.*

## Session 5

*Session 5 was good in that I was able to reinforce my intentions of focusing on the positive aspects of my career during a job interview. I could move away from feelings of resentment and a draining of self-esteem from the layoff. I visualized a friendly, positive, and effective job interview. And the reinforcement of my mentor, who praised me and reminded me of my past accomplishments, was helpful. I'm feeling more lighthearted, more positive, and more open to new possibilities. And I have a job interview tomorrow!*

## Session 6

*This last session was extremely fruitful. I did it after a yoga class, which I think helped me relax even further. I really began to internally voice the idea of reinventing myself. It's becoming an action plan rather than simply a concept. I realize I need to work on the self-destructive and negative voices in my head. I need to focus on finding the sources of that voice in order to understand it and overcome it. But I've made progress in that I also realize how it has been affecting my life journey. Even though I still worry about my future and other things (my financial health, etc.), I'm feeling freer and more positive about what I can accomplish. I'm able to turn my bad moods around more quickly and to shake off the useless feelings of despair that can grip me at any moment. I have bad days, but I know they won't last if I gain control over my feelings and emotions about myself. I need to start feeling like superwoman again, and I think I'm closer than I have been in a long time.*

As you can see, Sarah made great strides during her sessions. Even though she had been out of work for seven months and was emotionally beaten down and depressed when she began, within thirty days after her final session, she was back to work at a job she loved, thinking positively and feeling remarkably stronger. Sarah's experience promoted a journey to emotional health. If she can do it, you can too.

## Implementing Module 2

You're now ready to implement Module 2, the final three sessions in the Job-Loss Recovery Program. The module includes Basic Relaxation Skills plus the following scenarios: Mentally Rehearsing a Job Interview and Meeting Your Mentor. The following introduction to each of the scenario experiences will give you information and suggestions to add impact to the sessions. The complete script for Module 2 follows the introduction.

As with Module 1, I suggest recording the script for playback rather than reading it, to deepen and enhance the experience. Of course, you may choose to implement the module by silently reading the script rather than recording it and playing it back. However, it will be challenging to reach and maintain the deep focus and concentration needed to receive great benefit from the program if you attempt to immerse yourself in the experience while reading the script.

Keep in mind that you will better integrate the sessions by spacing them at least one day apart, as you did with Module 1.

A reminder: If you have chosen to implement each program scenario separately, rather than as a complete module, you'll find the scripts for each scenario included individually in appendix A. Begin with the mental-rehearsal scenario and then alternate it with the Mentor scenario until you've experienced each three times. And don't forget to begin each session with the Basic Relaxation Skills script.

## Module 2 Script Introduction

The second half of the program—Module 2—includes two main experiences, summarized in this section. As before, each session begins with the Basic Relaxation Skills script.

## *Mentally Rehearsing a Job Interview*

To begin Module 2, you will relax and go to your safe place. Again, the one-way window will be there, and you'll see yourself through the window, this time in an interview setting. If you have a real-life interview coming up, imagine that one. Otherwise, it can be any realistic interview that will take place in the future. You can then mentally direct the interview until it's satisfactory. An imaginary remote control device can be used as if the scene were a videotape. It can be stopped, rewound, or replayed, as you prefer.

This mental rehearsal segment of the guided visualization session will take only about five minutes, after which you will replay the perfect interview—without stopping—from beginning to end, feeling a sense of control and satisfaction. Your logical mind may tell you that five minutes isn't long enough to make an impact. But remember that my study participants had only five minutes, and many noted this segment as one of the most valuable in the program. Take as long as you like with this exercise, however. The goal is to feel confident and prepared.

Use both dissociated and associated perspectives in your mental rehearsals. Dissociation occurs when you are in your safe place, watching and directing the interview through the window. With association, you experience the interview by acting out a scene, actually playing the role as you did in the emotional-resolution segment of the program.

As you begin an interview—observing, critiquing, editing, and replaying—you'll find the process easier to do from a dissociated state.

If you find yourself being drawn into the scene at any time however, go with it. You can always move back to the dissociated state—step out of character, if you like—to edit the scene. When you're ready to play the entire scene without stopping, move into your character (the associated state) and give an enthusiastic performance that results in a job offer.

Although I've discussed mental rehearsal with a focus on interview preparation, it has extensive uses. Use your guided visualization sessions to rehearse and prepare for other job-search activities as well, such as making networking and referral calls.

## *Meeting Your Mentor*

When you finish interviewing, your Mentor will be waiting at the edge of your safe place for your invitation to enter. You will not need to create this being as you did your Future Self. You will be in a relaxed state and comfortably sense or imagine your Mentor. He or she may represent an aspect of yourself, information from your unconscious, or an inner guide—if your beliefs support that idea. Perhaps this person is someone you admire in real life, alive now or not. You can choose who you want to mentor you, or you can trust your creative unconscious to present the person who can help you most, whoever that is.

One thing is certain. Your Mentor knows you and supports you. You'll imagine greeting him or her and settling comfortably somewhere in your safe place. The two of you can consult about current directions and challenges, or you may ask for an analysis of your interviews and other job-search activities, whether they occurred in fact or were mentally rehearsed.

Unfortunately, although it's all-too-normal to listen to an inner critic tell you how undeserving and untalented you are, it may be initially uncomfortable for you to listen to an inner cheerleader and ally advise you about how successful you can be. But stick with it. It just takes faith and practice.

How will you communicate with one another while in your imaginary safe place? Some people talk, mentally, in the same way they might with a friend in reality. Or they share mental thoughts and feelings. Others derive a strong knowledge or a sense about what their Mentors communicate. Another useful approach is too simply allow thoughts to come into your mind as you sit in your supportive Mentor's presence, knowing you can examine the validity of those thoughts later. Experiment a little.

If the communications seem vague at first, don't stress. Open your senses of touch, smell, sound, and sight to this ally. The messages will become more clear with practice—another reason to experience each module several times. Also, as with your Future Self, a clear mental picture isn't necessary. Instead, you can create an underlying perception of your inner Mentor's guidance. This unseen image provides positive feedback and counsel when you relax and listen. Again, practice helps.

As soon as you complete a Module 2 session, make notes of any information and advice you received. Ask yourself three questions before following any advice accepted from your Mentor.

1.  *Would following the advice be in my best interest?*

    Let's say you're advised to call your former boss and give him or her a piece of your mind. Consider it carefully. This information sounds as if it may originate from a part of you that is feeling unresolved anger or resentment. Remember that a prospective employer may call your former boss to provide a reference for you. Therefore, following this advice may not be in your best interest.

2.  *Is the advice in harmony with my highest goals and principles?*

    Do your highest goals and principles provide for giving people a piece of your mind? If not, the answer is no.

3.  *Would it harm anyone?*

    Well, telling off your old boss could harm you, as I said, and possibly your boss as well.

In this scenario, I would send that Mentor away and ask for your wisest Mentor to appear instead. Remember, you are always in control.

The script for Module 2 of the guided visualization program follows. Remember, execute it three times over at least three days. You may want to return to chapter 3 first and review how to make the best use of the scripts.

## Module 2 Script: Relaxation, Mentally Rehearsing a Job Interview, Meeting Your Mentor

*Find a comfortable position. . . . Gently close your eyes. Begin by focusing on your breathing—inhaling deeply and exhaling fully. . . . Allow your abdomen to expand and contract as you breathe deep into your diaphragm. . . . And again . . . breathing in relaxation . . . and breathing out any tension in your body. . . . Inhale . . . exhale . . . relaxing more and more . . . becoming more calm with every breath. . . . Imagine any distracting thoughts drifting away. . . . For the moment, your mind is still . . . feeling calm and relaxed now . . . inhaling deeply . . . and exhaling.*

*Enjoy these few moments in peacefulness. . . . Notice the heaviness as your muscles begin to relax. . . . As I count down from five to one, allow yourself to become more and more relaxed. . . . Imagine all the anxiety flowing out of you as you relax deeper and deeper. . . . Five, four, going deeper, three, two, even deeper, and one. . . . Allow these feelings of tranquility to spread through your body. . . . You may notice a warm, heavy feeling coming over you, a sign of deep relaxation.*

*Move your attention to your feet. . . . Feel all the muscles in your feet and toes slowly relax, and begin to feel very loose and warm. . . . Allow the relaxation to spread into your calves as these muscles begin to feel loose, warm, and heavy. . . . Now release any tension you feel in your knees. . . . Now your thigh muscles begin to relax, all the tension releasing down, out of your feet, and into the earth. . . . This relaxing, peaceful feeling is a gift you're giving to yourself.*

*Now focus on your hips and abdomen. . . . Feel all the muscles loosening and relaxing. . . . Release any tension held there, allowing it to flow down and out of your body. . . . Now your back muscles are loosening, feeling warm. . . . Your neck and shoulders, a favorite place to hold burdens, are loosening and releasing any knots blocking you. . . . Continue to relax as you go deeper and deeper.*

*Move your attention to your arms, your upper and lower arms, and your hands. . . . Let go of any burdens and responsibilities. You can pick them up again later. . . . Sense your hands relaxing and warming as the tension flows out through your fingers. . . . Your jaw is now becoming loose and relaxed. . . . Your face is relaxing, feeling warm and heavy . . . all the muscles around your eyes, relaxing . . . all around your head, loosening and relaxing. . . . Feel the muscles releasing their knots, the anxiety and tension flowing down and out.*

*Take a few moments to scan through your body, noticing any remaining tension. . . . Release it now, letting it flow down and out. . . . Allow yourself to enjoy this relaxation and peacefulness.*

*Go even deeper into your inner world. . . . Imagine yourself in your special, safe place where you can be alone and at peace. . . . Remember that you can create and change your safe place any way you like. . . . It may be a secluded place in nature, such as an ocean beach with gentle waves lapping at the shore, or a forest clearing with the sounds of birds chirping . . . or perhaps it's a private garden with the intoxicating aroma and colors of your favorite flowers . . . any place where you feel comfortable and safe.*

*Look around this place. . . . Sense the shapes and colors coming into focus, becoming more and more clear. . . . Notice the time of day—perhaps the soft light of morning or the colorful setting sun. . . . Listen to the sounds around you. . . . Notice the fragrance in the air. . . . Feel the ground under your feet . . . and run your fingers through any body of water that might be there—perhaps a lily pond . . . or a trickling brook.*

*Make any changes you like; this is your place. . . . No one can come here without your invitation. . . . You are in control . . . and it feels good.*

*Once again, you move toward the large one-way window, with its view into your life. . . . But this time, take a seat in front of it. . . . Maybe there's an inviting armchair there, or a window-seat. . . . Notice a remote-control device within easy reach. . . . In a moment, you will look through the window and see yourself in a job interview or other job-search activity that demands peak performance. . . . You will be able to stop, revise, and replay anything you see or hear through the window by using the remote control to freeze the scene and then rewind and play a revised scene of your choice, watching as you continue the interview or other job-search activity with competence and confidence. . . . You may find yourself being drawn through the window, as you were in previous sessions, actually playing the role of yourself in the scene. . . . Feel free to do that. . . . Remember, though, you can step out of the scene and back into your safe place at any time to stop, revise, and replay it. . . . You'll finally play the entire scenario through without stopping, seeing and hearing yourself give a superb performance . . . understanding that this brief exercise can represent a full-length interview. . . . If you become distracted at any time, simply refocus and continue.*

*Now begin . . . seeing yourself talking easily with one or more people . . . noting the environment, the temperature of the room, feeling genuinely supported . . . hearing the questions asked and your answers, given confidently as you enjoy the process . . . perhaps feeling drawn through the window into the scene . . . stepping out of the scene and using your remote control to stop and revise any part of the interview . . . playing the new scene with you feeling calm and confident. . . . Noting the interviewer's positive response to you. . . . Continuing the process of interviewing, revising, and replaying. . . . Concluding the final scene.*

*Now, take the next two minutes to replay selected portions of the interview through without stopping. . . . Simply hit the high points and mentally fast-forward through the rest. . . . You are a star performer giving a top interview performance. . . . Your subconscious is getting the message that you want complete success. . . . Allow the current scene to successfully conclude (record silence for thirty seconds).*

*Know that you've done your best . . . . Realize you have the skills to overcome challenges and that you'll be wiser and stronger for having done so. . . . You are able do whatever is needed to reach your goals. . . . Imagine yourself moving ahead in time to when you have the new position you want. . . . Sense it in as much detail as you can. . . . How will it feel to have successfully achieved your goal? Feel those feelings now . . . the satisfaction and accomplishment. . . . Allow it to sink deep within (record silence for thirty seconds).*

*Finding yourself back in your safe place. . . . A slight movement out of the corner of your mental eye draws your attention and, as you look around, you notice someone waiting in the shadows at the edge of your safe place. . . . You nod in invitation, sensing it's not your Future Self this time and, as you approach one another, you become aware of a radiant light emanating from all around this being and wisdom in those eyes that seem to know you well. . . . Maybe you recognize this person. . . . Perhaps it's someone who has been a mentor or coach to you in the past—a relative perhaps, or a respected friend, living now or not. . . . Or perhaps it is someone you don't readily recognize. . . . Nevertheless, there is something familiar and comforting about those kind eyes and their powerful presence.*

*Welcome this Mentor into your safe place. . . . And, as you find a comfortable place to settle for a while, you may sit silently, being warmed in their supportive, loving presence. . . . Perhaps your Mentor will communicate with you through words . . . perhaps thoughts, images, or symbols . . . or some other unique way. . . . It doesn't matter. Simply drink it in. . . . You may use this time together for counsel and discussion of your current challenges and opportunities. . . . Perhaps you receive an assessment of the interviews you've mentally practiced, or other job-search activities. . . . If advice is offered and it feels right to you, accept it with gratitude. . . . It's your choice (record silence for a minute or more).*

*Sense the beauty of your own life's journey from this new perspective, the magnificence of your own growth and development. . . . Perhaps you see a larger plan, new directions, and new opportunities. . . . Perhaps your destiny is a choice after all. . . . And now, it's time to say goodbye. . . . As your Mentor departs, know that you may return here and meet again anytime you like.*

*In a moment you will come back to full awareness of the room where your journey began, feeling relaxed and refreshed. . . . The count from five to one will help you return. . . . Five . . . beginning to return . . . four . . . sensing the feelings in your body . . . three . . . sensing the environment around you . . . two . . . beginning to move around . . . and one. . . . When you are ready, open your eyes and return, feeling awake and refreshed. . . . Take a few slow, deep breaths. Stretch if you like, and enjoy the moment.*

*After Completing Module 2*

When you've completed Module 2 three times over three or more days, rate your visualization experiences once again with the following scale.

---

# Evaluating the Impact

The statements listed below refer to your program-session experiences. Using the following scale, from 1 to 7, with "I agree not at all" being 1 to "I agree extremely" being 7, place the corresponding number to the left of each of the following statements.

    1          2          3          4          5      6          7

\_\_\_\_    Overall, in my session(s), I felt my emotions deeply.

\_\_\_\_    Overall, the images in my session(s) were vivid and specific.

\_\_\_\_    My focus and involvement in the session(s) were very deep.

\_\_\_\_    My experience of relaxation in my session(s) has been deep.

\_\_\_\_    My sessions(s) were highly meaningful to me.

\_\_\_\_    **Total your score here.**

The total score amount is to be used for comparison only. You want to see an upward trend in subsequent scores over the course of the program. As your scores increase, expect the positive impact of the program experiences to increase as well.

---

Remember, the total score is to be used for comparison only. Compare your total score and individual ratings on each item with those you noted after completing Module 1. How have your ratings changed? Are you able to focus more easily now? Are your images clearer than when you began the program? Are you relaxing more deeply? If yes, these are some of the indications that your visualization skills have improved.

Next, complete the following Level of Distress Questionnaire and the Level of Confidence Questionnaire one more time, and total your scores on each.

# Level of Distress Questionnaire

The statements listed below refer to your inner feelings in regard to your job loss. Using the following scale from 1 to 10, insert the number that most closely reflects your current feelings and state of mind.

| 1 | 2 | 3 | 4 | 5 | 6 | 7 | 8 | 9 | 10 |
|---|---|---|---|---|---|---|---|---|----|
| *Never* | | *Sometimes* | | | *Frequently* | | *Most of the Time* | | |

_____ I have trouble focusing on what I am doing.

_____ I feel anxious

_____ I feel frustrated.

_____ I have waves of distressing feelings.

_____ I am reminded of my job loss often.

_____ I try to ignore my feelings about my job loss.

_____ I feel depressed.

_____ I have trouble staying motivated.

_____ I feel angry and/or resentful.

_____ I have trouble sleeping because I keep thinking about my job loss.

_____ I feel fearful.

_____ Any reminder brings back stressful feelings. I have troubling dreams about my job loss.

For this final statement, use a 1 to 10 scale but, this time, 1 indicates Strongly Disagree and 10 means Strongly Agree. Insert the number that most closely reflects your current belief, as is relevant to your job loss.

_____ Little can be done to change my job-related problems

_____ **Total your score here.**

This score represents your current level of distress about your job loss and is for comparison purposes only.

# Level of Confidence Questionnaire

Using the following scale from 1 to 10, insert the number that most closely reflects your confidence in your ability to perform that task.

1     2     3     4     5     6     7     8     9     10

*Not Confident*       *Moderately Confident*       *Highly Confident*

I can

\_\_\_\_\_     manage the demands created by my job loss.

\_\_\_\_\_     use my social network to obtain job leads.

\_\_\_\_\_     do what it takes to schedule job interviews.

\_\_\_\_\_     perform successfully in a job interview.

\_\_\_\_\_     manage my emotions while unemployed.

\_\_\_\_\_     see my job loss in a more positive light.

\_\_\_\_\_     learn something from my job-loss experience.

\_\_\_\_\_     concentrate my thoughts and efforts on my job search.

\_\_\_\_\_     **Total your score here.**

This score represents your current level of confidence related to your job loss and is for comparison purposes only.

Most people find a substantial decrease in their overall score on the Level of Distress Questionnaire. This is a sign of closure and a return to emotional health.

Note the statement at the bottom of the Level of Distress Questionnaire, "Little can be done to change my job-related problems." The statement reflects your new sense of control, and the score typically decreases several points or more following the program's completion—a good thing.

It's also usual to find a great increase in the overall score on the Level of Confidence Questionnaire. This reflects regained self-assurance about being able to effectively handle the issues and circumstances surrounding job loss and job search. As I explained in the beginning, both questionnaires were included so you could see tangible documentation of your achievements while implementing the Job-Loss Recovery Program.

If you haven't yet improved your levels on the questionnaires to a degree that feels comfortable to you, go back to the program modules and spend more time with them as needed. As a further aid, the next chapter's discussion of beliefs and blockages may be especially helpful.

After you've completed six sessions, you may want to go back to one or more of the scripts to focus on individually. You can spend as much time as you choose with each scenario. For example, if you have interviews scheduled, you may want to practice them with the mental rehearsal scenario to boost your confidence and maximize your performance on the interviews.

Congratulations! You've completed the Job-Loss Recovery Program. But many more achievements are possible by using your new visualization skills. In chapter 9, I explain how to bust through the limiting beliefs, emotional contracts, and resistances that can block each of us from achieving our greatest dreams and joys.

# Chapter 9

## *Breaking Your Barriers*

*Some people say, "I'll believe it when I see it." I prefer to say, "I'll see it when I believe it."*

—Dr. Robert Schuller

As you implemented the Job-Loss Recovery Program, the use of desire, expectation, and imagination helped to create unparalleled success. The program works. Many people have proved that over and over.

Yet you may have personal barriers that block your way. Three tactics can aid in breaking those barriers and achieving positive results.

1. Quickly identify and change your limiting beliefs.

2. Break negative emotional contracts with others.

3. Discover and learn from your resistances.

### *Quickly Identify and Change Limiting Beliefs*

First, examine your attitudes and beliefs regarding work and achieving goals; then change any that limit and impede your success. It's easier than it sounds. Our attitudes and beliefs determine what we think and how we feel. And our thoughts and feelings, in turn, determine the decisions and choices we make. So, if your decisions and choices aren't yielding the desired results in your job search, examine the underlying beliefs. Do they empower you or frustrate you?

Remember when I told you about that old belief of mine that success in life doesn't come without a struggle? My hard-working parents worried and struggled to make a good life for their children and therefore became my role models for struggle. They became successful business-people in their community but not without struggling through difficult times. It seemed as if nothing came easily. With no conscious awareness, I listened and observed them, coming to believe this reality was the way it was for everyone. As I grew up, my life experiences consistently validated this belief. My achievements were always preceded by struggle and worry.

Thus, the belief I subconsciously developed as a child shaped the way I viewed and experienced the world. This is how many beliefs are formed.

> ## EXPERIENCES ARE FILTERED THROUGH OUR BELIEFS.

We experience reality through the filter of our beliefs. In other words, we unconsciously screen out anything that doesn't conform to those beliefs. What each of us actually experiences is the reality that we believe is possible and true. Other potential experiences don't make it through the filter into reality. For instance, I once knew a man who believed most people were rude and inconsiderate; it seemed to him that only rude and inconsiderate people passed through his life. In truth, however, when a considerate person crossed his path (as I observed more than once), he simply didn't notice. Had he done so, the experience would have challenged his belief that all people were rude and inconsiderate. And none of us wants our beliefs questioned. We want to be right more than we want to be challenged.

Another lesson learned by one of Spencer Johnson's little characters in *Who Moved My Cheese* (1998) is worth noting: "Old beliefs do not lead you to new cheese". He realized that his new beliefs were encouraging new behaviors. When you change what you believe, you change what you do.

At one point in my thirties, a teacher I admired talked about the critical role of beliefs in human experiences. She said life was never meant to be difficult. Her comments prompted me to begin examining my own limiting beliefs relating to areas of my life that weren't working as well as I would have liked, and I discovered techniques to change them. What a difference it made in my life. That's why I'd like to show you exactly how to do it for yourself.

## Exercise: Identify Your Limiting Beliefs

Experiencing job loss challenges personal beliefs. Most Americans believe that life is supposed to be fair, and that hard work begets rewards. When the chair is pulled out from under you, these beliefs in fairness, loyalty, and reward are in question.

You may also recognize some of these common limiting beliefs that can block success: "I never get any breaks," "I'm not good enough," "This won't work," and "Change is bad."

In the following guided visualization exercise, you will be guided back through a timeline of the past year of your life to help you identify undesirable events and reveal any limiting belief that may underlie them.

Have your Journal handy. Select a location where you won't be disturbed for fifteen or twenty minutes.

*Find a comfortable position. . . . Gently close your eyes. Begin by focusing on your breathing—inhaling deeply . . . and exhaling. . . . Breathe deep into your diaphragm . . . breathing in relaxation . . . and breathing out any tension in your body. . . . Inhale . . . exhale . . . relaxing more and more. . . . Imagine any distracting thoughts drifting away. . . . For the moment, your mind is still . . . feeling calm and relaxed now . . . inhaling deeply . . . and exhaling. . . . Allow these feelings of relaxation to spread through your body. . . . Notice the heaviness as your muscles begin to relax.*

*Imagine yourself in your special, safe place where you are alone and at peace. . . . Sense the shapes and colors coming into focus, becoming more and more clear. . . . Listen to the sounds of nature around you. . . . Notice the fragrance in the air, the smell of pine trees or colorful wildflowers. . . . Notice the time of day—perhaps the soft light of morning or the colorful setting sun. . . . Make any changes you like. . . . You are in control. . . . Let any distracting thoughts float away, as you go even deeper.*

*Find a comfortable place to recline in your safe place, and close your mental eyes. . . . Imagine you're walking back through a timeline of the past year of your life . . . observing events and results of your efforts as they occurred. . . . For the moment, you're interested in only the unwanted happenings that related to your work life or job search. Start with the present and slowly walk through the past year, month by month. As you notice an undesirable incident, walk a little further back, to the decisions and the choices you made leading up to that work-related situation. . . . Simply observe. Don't become emotionally involved. Take a couple of minutes to do that now.*

*Now, walk a little further back through the timeline to recognize what you were thinking and feeling just before you made those decisions and choices. . . . Look deeply into yourself and be honest. . . . What were your thoughts at the time, and what were you feeling? Simply observe. Take a minute to do that now.*

*Finally, what was your most prominent attitude at the time? And what is, most likely, the belief supporting that attitude . . . the belief that, directly or indirectly, could be capable of having promoted the unwanted result? . . . You may consider several possible beliefs before one of them feels most accurate. Do that now.*

*When you've identified a limiting belief, walk even further back through the timeline, perhaps even beyond a year . . . looking for other unwanted events in your life that originated with that very belief . . . looking for a pattern of three or more events. Do that now.*

*Know that everyone has limiting beliefs, and that you are on the way to recognizing yours . . . and replacing them with positive beliefs that will support and promote your goals and dreams.*

*When you're ready, come back to full awareness of the room where your journey began, feeling refreshed and alert. Take a few slow, deep breaths, and open your eyes.*

Immediately take some time to write about what you've learned. In your Journal:

1.  Choose the event or result that impacted you most during the exercise. Name it, and describe it briefly.

2.  Write the decisions and choices you made leading up to it.

3.  Write about the thoughts and feelings that preceded those decisions and choices.

4.  Write the underlying belief that feels most accurate. Use as few words as possible. Be succinct.

Let's use the above process with the following example. Assume you had participated in four progressive interviews with a company you liked. After the third interview, you had been informed that only one other candidate vied with you for final consideration. You knew a little about the other candidate, and you thought they had more impressive qualifications for the position than you. You remember feeling disappointed and deciding they would probably get the offer. They did.

On your paper, you would note the following:

1. The event or *result*: interview rejection.

2. The prior *decision* you made internally: "The other candidate will get the job offer."

3. Your *thoughts*: "Their qualifications are more impressive than mine"; and your *feelings*: disappointment and perhaps fear of failure.

4. "I'm not good enough" is a *belief* that could easily have led to these decisions, thoughts, feelings, and results. You need not make an absolute determination, however, based on one result. Look for a pattern of results before concluding that a particular belief is limiting your success.

Repeat the above procedure until you're confident you've identified all the work-related beliefs that hold you back.

If you like, you can use the timeline to go back even further in your life, to the time you first acquired each belief. It's not necessary to do so, however, because *you can always change a limiting belief without knowing its origin.*

---

If you're not sure whether a certain belief is healthy or not, ask yourself:

- Does it empower or frustrate me in reaching my goals and dreams?

- Does it make me feel good or bad? Understand that a limiting belief can feel comfortable, like an old shoe.

- Does it protect me in a positive way or not?

If you decide it's no longer in your best interest to hold on to the belief, then it's time to release it and adopt a more constructive one.

> CHANGE YOUR BELIEF TO CHANGE YOUR
> EXPERIENCE.

## Exercise: Changing Your Limiting Beliefs

Once you acknowledge a limiting belief that impedes your positive life choices, examine it. How can you change or reverse the negative impact on your career development? Create a new belief to disprove the old—something that will totally contradict that old conviction. That done, mentally express the old belief in one short sentence. Then, in the first person, express the new belief positively, also in a short sentence, using as few words as possible.

For instance, if I rephrased my old belief, "I can't achieve success without struggle," to "Anything I desire comes to me with ease," I could mentally state: "I now release the belief that I can't achieve success without struggle. And I now believe anything I desire comes to me with ease." Repeat it several times for deeper impact. Remind yourself whenever you need to that "Anything I desire comes to me with ease."

If you're thinking, "Changing my beliefs can't be this easy," let me point out that you've just expressed a belief you may want to examine.

I learned a second technique many years ago and have used it successfully over and over again. It is implemented in the next exercise script by the use of pictures and metaphors—both of which are easily understood by your new ally, your subconscious. When you have identified a limiting belief, you will go to your safe place and find your way along a path, into a cave. Deep in the cave you'll find a vast, softly lit cavern. In the center will stand a pedestal holding a book titled "My Book of Beliefs." You will open the book to see a limiting belief written on the page and will then be guided through a procedure to replace it with a new belief of your choice. Give it a try.

*Find a comfortable position. . . . Gently close your eyes. Begin by focusing on your breathing—inhaling deeply . . . and exhaling fully. . . . Breathe deep into the diaphragm . . . breathing in relaxation . . . and breathing out any tension in your body. . . . Inhale . . . exhale . . . relaxing more and more. . . . Imagine any distracting thoughts drifting away. . . . For the moment, your mind is still . . . feeling calm and relaxed now . . . inhaling deeply . . . and exhaling. . . . Allow these feelings of relaxation to spread through your body. . . . Notice the heaviness as your muscles begin to relax.*

*Imagine yourself in your special, safe place where you are alone and at peace. . .*

*. Sense the shapes and colors coming into focus, becoming more and more clear. . . . Listen to the sounds of nature around you. . . . Notice the fragrance in the air, the smell of pine trees or colorful wildflowers. . . . Notice the time of day, perhaps the soft light of morning or the colorful setting sun. . . Make any changes you like. . . . You are in control. . . . Let any distracting thoughts float away, as you go even deeper.*

*Begin walking along a winding path that you hadn't seen before. . . . As you round a bend, come to the mouth of a cave that seems to beckon you inside. . . . Curious, you walk deep into the cave . . . toward a soft glow ahead . . . and come to a vast cavern, softly lit by candles all around. . . . Notice a pedestal standing in the center of the room. . . . On it sits a large, dusty book. . . . The cover reads, "My Book of Beliefs."*

*Walk over to the book and open it to a page on which is written an old belief you intend to release. . . . Pick up a black marking pen from a small table by the pedestal, and draw a large X on the page over the words. . . . Put the marker down and tear out the page. . . . Then rip the page into pieces and burn them in a nearby receptacle. . . . Feel the freedom and exhilaration of finally releasing the belief.*

*Look back at the book. Behind the ripped page you tore out is a blank page. . . . Pick up the marker and sense the satisfaction of writing your new belief on the page. . . . Mentally read it aloud in the candlelit cavern. . . . Feel its impact and allow it to sink in. . . . Now close the book. . . . Know that you have replaced an old, negative belief with a new, positive one. . . . Allow it to be done.*

*When you are ready, come back to awareness of the room where your journey began, feeling refreshed and alert. Take a few slow, deep breaths, and open your eyes.*

---

Can you really let go of an old belief and adopt a new one that easily? You decide. *Conscious beliefs are always a choice.*

## Break Negative Emotional Contracts with Others

Another tactic to break your emotional barriers is to examine any undesirable emotional contracts you may have made with others in your younger, more impressionable years.

Throughout childhood and early-adult years, people often unconsciously make agreements with others they depend upon, such as parents and siblings. It's done instinctively and out of self-preservation.

They might be contracts of love, contracts of anxiety and worry, or contracts of hate and hurt. These unwritten contracts often render us unable to use our tools of manifestation—desire, imagination, and expectation—to our fullest potential.

Contracts of love are often motivated out of a desire to hold on to the love of parents. As a way to ensure that we get our parents' love, we fulfill their desires, not ours. I once had a client, Linda, who followed in her father's footsteps by getting into sales. From adolescence on, her father, a successful sales manager, had strongly encouraged her in that direction. Wanting very much to please him, Linda sought and accepted a sales position as soon as she graduated from college. Although unaware of it at the time, she had made an emotional contract with her father that went something like this: "I'll become the person you want me to be and, in return, you'll always love and accept me." She attempted to fulfill her father's desires for her, never asking herself what her own desires might be.

Linda did well enough in sales for a few years, but her heart was not in it. When a layoff followed a company merger, she immediately began seeking another sales position. But she always found something wrong. She didn't like the product, the compensation wasn't good enough, they didn't offer the right territory, or she simply didn't get the offer. I asked Linda how she happened to become interested in sales and she blurted out, "I was never interested in sales." She seemed surprised at her own response, and as we talked further, Linda realized she had never been interested in any other vocation, either. As long as she could remember, she'd accepted that she would have a sales career. She had allowed her father to choose for her. When she related the story to me, she felt anger toward him. Later, she recognized her own willingness to accept the choice and turned her anger inward.

Before she could move on to success in fully gaining freedom of choice, Linda had to first break her emotional contract with her father and resolve the anger and forgive both her father and herself. Once she had done that, she gained the freedom to move in new directions.

Ask yourself whose desires you attempt to fulfill. Yours or someone else's?

Other emotional contracts include a parental promise or a societal obligation. For example you may have internalized a promise you once made to your father: "Out of respect and love for you, I will never become more successful than you." If this feels very familiar, you may have to break a similar agreement to achieve the level of success you want.

To determine what emotional contracts you may harbor, evaluate your happiness and feelings of success prior to losing your job. Did you feel misdirected or unsatisfied? If so, why? Look beyond the obvious. Look for consistent work patterns rather than simply at your last position.

Honestly examine your relationships with parents and siblings. And, if you feel you might have a work-related emotional contract, then you probably do. Keep in mind that I'm talking about limiting and undesirable contracts, not the kind that spur you on to success and fulfillment.

---

## Exercise: Breaking Negative
## Emotional Contracts

When you discover a contract you want to break, do it with ease and sensibility. Here's how: In the following guided visualization script, you will imagine severing a visible negative connection that you've emotionally contracted with someone. As always, select a location where you won't be disturbed.

*Find a comfortable position. . . . Gently close your eyes. . . . Begin by focusing on your breathing . . . inhaling deeply . . . and exhaling fully. . . . Breathe deep into your diaphragm . . . breathing in relaxation . . . and breathing out any tension in your body. . . . Inhale . . . exhale . . . relaxing more and more. . . . Imagine any distracting thoughts drifting away. . . . For the moment, your mind is still . . . feeling calm and relaxed now . . . inhaling deeply . . . and exhaling. . . . Allow these feelings of relaxation to spread through your body. . . . Notice the heaviness, as your muscles begin to relax.*

*Imagine yourself in your special, safe place where you are alone and at peace. . . . Sense the shapes and colors coming into focus, becoming more and more clear. . . . Listen to the sounds of nature around you. . . . Notice the fragrance in the air, the smell of pine trees or colorful wildflowers. . . . Notice the time of day, perhaps the soft light of morning or the colorful setting sun. . . . Make any changes you like. . . . You are in control. . . . Let any distracting thoughts float away as you go even deeper.*

*Think of the person with whom you want to break the emotional contract . . . and think about the contract itself. . . . Has it helped you in some way? . . . If so, how? . . . Perhaps you did receive more love and now feel grateful, as a result. . . . Or has it impeded your growth and success? . . . If it has, forgive yourself for making the agreement in the first place. . . . You did the best you could at the time. . . . Feel your commitment to break this contract that is no longer in your best interest.*

*Now invite into your safe place the person with whom you made that agreement so long ago. . . . This person will come, whether currently living or not. . . . Sense them tentatively walking toward you, silently standing a comfortable distance in front of you. . . . Notice a visible connection between you, one you never saw before, emanating from somewhere in your body and stretching across and into the body of the person in front of you. . . . Perhaps it's made of string or cord. . . . It doesn't matter.*

*If you'd like to say something to this person, do so now. . . . Perhaps you say that although you still feel love, it's time to free yourself from the limiting emotional contract you made so long ago.*

*Now pick up a pair of scissors that lies nearby, and cut easily through the connecting substance. . . . Watch as the person standing in front of you floats up . . . and fades into the distance. . . . Know now that a limiting emotional contract binding you together no longer exists . . . and you may now freely continue a relationship with that person or not, as you choose.*

*Think what your life will be like without this blocking emotional contract. . . . What new choices can you make? . . . In what new ways can you apply your skills? . . . Feel the sense of freedom.*

*When you are ready, come back to awareness of the room where your journey began, feeling refreshed and alert. Take a few slow, deep breaths, and enjoy the moment.*

---

Repeat the exercise with each emotional contract you have. You'll discover that it works well. In fact, you may find that the real person with whom you've broken the contract will actually recognize something is different right away. I know a woman who broke an emotional contract in this manner with her mother—to whom she hadn't spoken in many months. The very next day she received a phone call from her mother, demanding to know what had happened!

*The Job-Loss Recovery Program Guide*

## *Discover and Learn from Your Resistances*

The third tactic you can use to create greater success is to recognize and learn about your own resistances to change. You may unconsciously resist the very change you consciously want. In other words, you may say you want change but act as if don't. Why would you do that?

*Resistances* are psychological defenses or barriers that protect us from thoughts or feelings that may be too difficult to tolerate. Being resistant is not bad or wrong. Unconscious defenses help shut off past, unresolved grief, fear, and other emotions to prevent them from interfering with normal, day-to-day functions. The problem arises when defenses strengthen to the point of barricading a change you really want.

For example, you may subconsciously resist using the techniques offered by this Job-Loss Recovery Program. A part of you may object to the program or to continuing on your current path.

Whatever your underlying resistances, you will want to learn to recognize them in order to determine what to do about them.

Resistances take many forms, but you may be experiencing resistance *if you*

- Don't act on one or more of the insights you gain while implementing the Job-Loss Recovery Program.
- Feel unusually anxious or uncomfortable while implementing the program.
- Do only the relaxation segment of the program.
- Skip over the emotional-closure scenario of the program.
- Experience extreme difficulty with any of the program's scenarios.
- Allow everything else to take priority over your participation in the program.

### Exercise: Learning from Your Resistance

In the following guided visualization scenario, you will converse with an image of your resistance and explore why it might be there and how it got there. What could it be protecting you from? What does it need in order to allow the change you want? I adapted the exercise from a script by Dr. Martin Rossman in *Guided Imagery for Self-Healing* (2000).

As always, select a location where you won't be disturbed.

*Find a comfortable position. . . . Gently close your eyes. . . . Begin by focusing on your breathing . . . inhaling deeply . . . and exhaling fully. . . . Breathe deep into your diaphragm . . . breathing in relaxation . . . and breathing out any tension in your body. . . . Inhale . . . exhale . . . relaxing more and more. . . . Imagine any distracting thoughts drifting away. . . . For the moment, your mind is still . . . feeling calm and relaxed now . . . inhaling deeply . . . and exhaling. Allow these feelings of relaxation to spread through your body. . . . Notice the heaviness as your muscles begin to relax.*

*Imagine yourself in your special, safe place where you are alone and at peace. . . . Sense the shapes and colors coming into focus, becoming more and more clear. . . . Listen to the sounds of nature around you. . . . Notice the fragrance in the air, the smell of pine trees or colorful wildflowers. . . . Notice the time of day, perhaps the soft light of morning or the colorful setting sun. . . . Make any changes you like. . . . You are in control. . . . Let any distracting thoughts float away as you go even deeper.*

*Find the spot in your safe place where you feel most calm, most aware, and become comfortable in that spot. . . . Sense the quiet calm you feel here.*

*When you're ready, ask yourself if any element of you has an objection to or concern about your continuing on the path of recovery with the Job-Loss Recovery Program or with your current job search. . . . Simply ask, quietly listen, and wait for an answer.*

*If there is no response, begin to imagine yourself taking the next step in the Job-Loss Recovery Program or job search. . . . Invite any element of you that may have an objection to appear in your safe place so you can understand its concerns.*

*Watch as an image forms to represent this element of you. . . . It may look like you or not. . . . Thank the image for revealing itself . . . and ask it to share its objections with you, in a way you can understand. . . . Ask any questions you may have, to clarify its concerns (pause).*

*Think about what you are learning from this part of yourself. . . . Does it make sense to you? . . . Does the image appear fearful or angry? . . . Why? . . . Ask it what it needs to drop its opposition to your goals. . . . Listen to the answer (pause).*

*Invite your Mentor to join you, and welcome them into your safe place. . . . Tell your Mentor about the objections of this element of yourself. . . . Perhaps your*

*Mentor can suggest some ways to meet its needs and free you to move ahead unobstructed. . .*

*Listen closely to your Mentor's ideas and guidance. . . . Ask any questions you may have. . . . The image wants to have its needs met, and it also wants to be on your team rather than the opposition's.*

*Share with the image the suggestions that feel reasonable to you. . . . Can its needs be met in these ways? . . . Watch and listen for a response. . . . If the answer is yes, imagine implementing the suggested actions . . . with a successful outcome.*

*If no ideas are forthcoming or accepted, ask both the element of yourself and your Mentor if they would search the unconscious for creative solutions . . . and meet again in a few days to discuss the new ideas. . . . Arrange a meeting time.*

*When you're ready, come back to awareness of the room where your journey began, feeling refreshed and alert. Take a few slow, deep breaths, and enjoy the moment.*

---

Immediately take some time to write about what you've learned.

---

What was the image like? Were you able to recognize your resistive self? If so,

- Could you relate to its objections?
- Do you feel you can remedy them well enough, and will you take action to do that?
- What actions will you take?
- What did you learn from the experience?

Remain alert for ideas and insights that may come to you over the next few days as you go about your daily activities. Above all, don't judge yourself for having inner objections to your success. It's perfectly normal for a part of you to resist, and becoming aware of the conflicting emotions is, in itself, taking a positive step. But now that you are aware of your objections, you may be able to make some new allies of the different elements of yourself.

In her audiotape program, *How to Live the Life You Love* (1994), Barbara Sher presents an interesting alternative concept designed to deal with resistance. Her idea is to bypass your resistance, no matter what its origin or makeup. Sher suggests breaking up the task or project into small, palatable units, making it a comfortable process and thereby less resistive.

For instance, if you find yourself procrastinating in reading or listening to the Job-Loss Recovery Program modules, take the following steps:

1. First, sit or recline comfortably for three or four minutes while slowing your breathing and imagining something relaxing, such as walking on a deserted beach. If you have difficulty maintaining the process for that long, start with one or two minutes and gradually extend the time over a few days.

2. Implement this process on a planned schedule in order to develop the habit of doing a little something from the program every day.

3. After you've worked up to four minutes, move to the program's relaxation script and complete the full-body relaxation, without the safe place portion, once a day for two or three days.

4. Then add the safe place to your routine.

5. You should then be ready to add the program modules as described in this book.

You get the idea. The key is to start small, which encourages participation. It's important to be comfortable with the process and not overwhelmed by it.

To sum up:

- You've learned to identify and change the limiting beliefs that block your success.

- You can now recognize and break negative emotional contracts with others.

- You can work in positive ways with your resistances.

You can now break the barriers that have kept you from the level of success you want and have learned to deal effectively with any new ones that might arise in the future. Congratulations!

# Chapter 10

## *Your New Vision:*
## *Making a Living with No Emotional Barriers*

*Go confidently in the direction of your dreams. Live the life you have imagined.*

—Henry David Thoreau

### *Review Your Accomplishments*

Let's take stock of how far you've come since first opening this book. You've learned how to use guided visualization to

- Relax and manage stressful symptoms.
- Reach closure on the loss of your job.
- Increase confidence and self-esteem.
- Improve job-search performance.
- Renew hope and build resilience.
- Identify and change beliefs that limit success.
- Break unwanted emotional contracts with others.
- Discover and work with your resistances.
- Use desire, expectation, and imagination to promote success in all you do.

You're now prepared to land the job of your choice, quickly and easily.

### *Create a New Vision for Your Life*

What if every worker in the world had these new skills? Can you imagine what the world would be like if billions of people could quickly process and resolve all their emotional baggage, if billions could dissolve their inner barriers to success and happiness in addition to the emotional obstructions between themselves and others?

New realities have always started with dreams and visions. What are yours? *Allow yourself to dream.*

Think of every person as a pebble dropped in a lake. No matter where in the lake the pebble is dropped, it creates ripples that span out in all directions and are felt throughout the lake to every shore. In the same way, the actions we take as individuals create impact that is felt, directly or indirectly, by people we don't even know. The dreams you dream, with desire and expectation of success, will attract opportunities for your consideration, action, and manifestation.

John Lennon must have known about the power of the imagination when he wrote the lyrics: "Imagine all the people living life in peace. You may say I'm a dreamer, but I'm not the only one. I hope someday you'll join us, and the world will be as one."

# Appendix A

## Guided Visualization Scripts: Individual Program Scenarios

If you selected the alternate program structure (Choice B), you will use the following five guided visualization scripts to implement the Job-Loss Recovery Program. Begin each session with the Basic Relaxation Skills script that appears first. Follow that with one of the four succeeding script scenarios in the order given. You may want to review the section in chapter 6 to see exactly how each session is organized. Remember to space your twelve sessions over twelve or more days.

As you read through the scripts, mentally or aloud, read slowly, and pause where you see the dots ( . . . ) to experience the suggested imagery. Follow a similar procedure, reading aloud, to customize and record the scripts.

### *Script: Basic Relaxation Skills*

*Find a comfortable position. . . . Gently close your eyes. Begin by focusing on your breathing—inhaling deeply . . . and exhaling fully. . . . Allow your abdomen to expand and contract as you breathe deep into your diaphragm. . . . And again . . . breathing in relaxation . . . and breathing out any tension in your body. . . Inhale . . . exhale . . . relaxing more and more . . . becoming more calm with every breath. . . . Imagine any distracting thoughts drifting away. . . . For the moment, your mind is still . . . feeling calm and relaxed now . . . inhaling deeply . . . and exhaling.*

*Enjoy these few moments in peacefulness. . . . Notice the heaviness as your muscles begin to relax. . . . As I count down from five to one, allow yourself to become more and more relaxed. . . . Imagine all the anxiety flowing out of you as you relax deeper and deeper. . . . Five, four, going deeper, three, two, even deeper, and one. . . . Allow these feelings of tranquility to spread through your body. . . . You may notice a warm, heavy feeling coming over you, a sign of deep relaxation.*

*Now move your attention to your feet. . . . Feel all the muscles in your feet and toes slowly relax and begin to feel very loose and warm. . . . Allow the relaxation to spread into your calves as these muscles begin to feel loose, warm, and heavy. . . . Now release any tension you feel in your knees. . . . Now feel your thigh muscles begin to relax, all the tension releasing down, out of your feet and into the earth. . . . This relaxing, peaceful feeling is a gift you're giving to yourself.*

*Now focus on your hips and abdomen. . . . Feel all the muscles loosening and relaxing. . . . Release any tension held there, allowing it to flow down and out of your body. . . . Now your back muscles are loosening, feeling warm. . . . Your neck and shoulders, a favorite place to hold burdens, are loosening and releasing any knots blocking you. . . . Continue to relax as you go deeper and deeper.*

*Move your attention to your arms, your upper and lower arms, and your hands. . . . Let go of any burdens and responsibilities. You can pick them up again later. . . . Sense your hands relaxing and warming as the tension flows out through your fingers. . . . Now focus on your jaw, sensing it becoming loose and relaxed. . . . Now your face is relaxing, feeling warm and heavy . . . all the muscles around your eyes, relaxing . . . all around your head, loosening and relaxing. . . . Feel the muscles releasing their knots, the anxiety and tension flowing down and out.*

*Now, take a few moments to scan through your body, noting any remaining tension. . . . Release it now, and let it flow down and out. . . . Allow yourself to enjoy this relaxation and peacefulness.*

*Relax even deeper. . . . Allow your mind to become calm and peaceful. . . . Remember, you can send thoughts and feelings drifting away. . . . Focus on your feelings of deep, peaceful relaxation.*

*Now go even deeper. . . . Imagine yourself in a very special and safe place where you can be alone and at peace. . . . You can create your safe place and change it any way you like at any time. . . . Maybe it's a secluded place in nature, such as an ocean beach with gentle waves lapping at the shore, or a forest clearing with the comforting sounds of birds . . . or perhaps a mountain meadow with a gentle breeze whispering through the wildflowers . . . any place where you feel comfortable and safe.*

*Look around your safe place. . . . Sense the shapes and colors coming into focus, becoming more and more clear. . . . Notice what time of day it is—perhaps the soft light of morning or the colorful setting sun. . . . Listen to the sounds of nature around you. . . Notice the fragrance in the air. . . . Feel the earth under your feet, or run your fingers through the water that might be there.*

*Make any changes you like; this is your place. . . . No one can come here without your invitation. . . . You are in control. . . . It feels good. . . . Let any distracting thoughts float away, as you go even deeper.*

## *Script: Emotional Closure*

Remember to begin your session with the Basic Relaxation Skills script.

*Now, out of the corner of your mental eye, something captures your attention, and you turn to see a large free-standing window somewhere in your safe place. . . . Curious, you move toward it and somehow know this is a one-way window into your world. . . . You can see through it to the other side, but no one can see you. . . . As you look through the window, a scene begins to come into focus. . . . You realize this is you at your former job . . . perhaps when you were told you would be let go. . . . You choose the scene.*

*Now feel yourself being gently drawn through the window and sense yourself there. . . . It may seem like a long time ago, or like yesterday. . . . Look around. . . . Listen to the sounds, perhaps of people talking or of computers or other equipment operating. . . . Mentally reach out and touch something in your environment. . . . Perhaps you slide your fingers across a desk. . . . How did you feel at the time? . . . Others, when laid off, have often felt shock at first, then anger or sadness, anxiety, fear, guilt, or even embarrassment. . . . How did you respond? What actions did you take? . . . Or did you do nothing? . . . Are you angry or resentful? . . . If you are, is it toward others? Or perhaps you're mad at yourself for being vulnerable and losing control of your career.*

*Now invite into your scene, if they're not already there, anyone to whom you want to express your thoughts and feelings without fear of retaliation. . . . Sense them with you, and greet them in your own way. . . . Notice their expressions, their clothing. . . . Remember how you felt, how you feel now. . . . Now set your intention on mentally saying anything you want to say but with no actual intent to harm anyone in reality. . . . As a symbol of your intention to harm no one, sense a protective shield or bubble around you and the other person or persons in your scene.*

*Mentally say what is on your mind. . . . Don't think about choosing your words carefully. . . . Simply express your feelings. . . . If you feel angry, abandoned, or betrayed, tell them about it as they listen intently to you. . . . If you have mixed feelings, express the ambivalence as well . . . perhaps the sadness of losing contact with friends . . . along with anticipation of new opportunities. . . . You may be surprised at some of the feelings that surface within you. . . . Anything you feel is okay. . . . Simply say anything you want. . . . Let it all go. . . . Reach deep within you and release it all. . . . It feels good to release what you have been holding onto. . . . You may feel a sense of relief.*

*Now, how would you prefer to have this person or these people respond to you? . . . Remember, you are writing the script. . . . Listen as they respond in exactly that way. . . . How does that feel? . . . Don't label it, simply feel it, allowing the feeling to wash over and through you.*

*Now, if you like, impose upon them whatever retribution you feel is fair and just . . . It's entirely your choice. . . . Now is your chance. . . . Perhaps you want them to get on their knees and beg your forgiveness. . . . Go for it. You are in control . . . and you're not intending harm to anyone in reality. . . . They do not resist or retaliate in anyway. . . . If they sincerely apologize, accept it or not, as you like . . . Forgive if you can do so honestly . . . only when you're ready.*

*Think of your safe place now, and find yourself there once again . . . perhaps with expanded perspective. . . . Maybe you discovered anger you hadn't realized was there. . . . Perhaps you surprised yourself by forgiving and feel a weight lifting off you. . . . You are learning more about who you are. . . . You know, too, that you are doing your best, and that new opportunities for work and growth are not limited . . . . If one passes, another will reveal itself. . . . You know that challenges are a part of life's journey and that you have the skills to successfully move through and beyond them.*

*In a moment, you will come back to full awareness of the room where your journey began, feeling relaxed and refreshed. . . . The count of three, two, and one will help you return. . . . Three . . . begin to return, sense the feelings in your body . . . two, sense the environment around you and begin to move around . . . and one. . . . When you are ready, open your eyes and return, feeling awake and refreshed. . . . Take a few slow, deep breaths, stretch if you like, and enjoy the moment.*

# Script: Meeting Your Future Self

Remember to begin your session with the Basic Relaxation Skills script.

*Out of the corner of your mental eye, you notice someone standing in shadow at the edge of your safe place. . . . Curious, you move closer. . . . This person looks amazingly like you, yet somehow different. . . . You realize now that this is you at some point in your future. . . . This Future Self represents the epitome of your potential self—the wisest, the most loving, the most happy and successful self you can become in this lifetime.*

*Invite your Future Self into your safe place . . . and as the figure slowly approaches . . . coming more into focus . . . look for details. . . . You may or may not see the image clearly—it doesn't matter. . . . Simply sense the essence and existence of this future you. . . . Sense the connection between you. . . . Greet one another in whatever way feels right for you, perhaps a touch or an embrace.*

*And now look into the eyes of this Future Self, and feel the warmth and loving support coming from one who truly knows you. . . . See your current life through the perspective of those wise, loving eyes. . . . Perhaps you get a sense of what you are truly capable of doing with your abilities in this lifetime. . . . Allow any feelings and images to wash over you. . . . Communicate with your Future Self now, either through words or in images or in a bodily sensing, in any way that feels right. . . . Perhaps you ask for insight into your progress with healing the emotional pain . . . or simply experience being in one another's presence. . . . Take the next minute to do that.*

*Know that you will overcome your current challenges and will be stronger and wiser for it. . . . Forgive yourself, as well as others, for past failures or disappointments. . . . Now imagine having received an offer for the position of your choice. . . . Feel the pleasure of having successfully completed your search . . . and imagine yourself celebrating with your loved ones.*

*Mentally feel the gentle squeeze of a hand on your arm as your Future Self reaches out to you with a gift. . . . It may be an object, a symbol, a word, or a thought . . . tangible or not. . . . Allow it be whatever it is. . . . If it feels right to do so, simply accept it. . . . If you don't understand it, that's all right. . . . For now, it's enough to know that it comes with love.*

*In a moment, you will come back to full awareness of the room where your journey began, feeling relaxed and refreshed. . . . The count of three, two, and one will help you return. . . . Three . . . begin to return, sense the feelings in your body . . . two, sense the environment around you and begin to move around . . . and one. . . . When you are ready, open your eyes and return, feeling awake and refreshed. . . . Take a few slow, deep breaths, stretch if you like, and enjoy the moment.*

## Script: Mentally Rehearsing a Job Interview

Remember to begin your session with the Basic Relaxation Skills script.

*Once again, you move toward the large one-way window, with its view into your life. . . . But this time, take a seat in front of it. . . . Maybe there's an inviting armchair there, or a window-seat. . . . Notice a remote-control device within easy reach. . . . In a moment, you will look through the window and see yourself in a job interview or other job-search activity that demands peak performance. . . . You will be able to stop, revise, and replay anything you see or hear through the window by using the remote control to freeze the scene and then rewind and play a revised scene of your choice, watching as you continue the interview or other job-search activity with competence and confidence. . . . You may find yourself being drawn through the window, as you were in previous sessions, actually playing the role of yourself in the scene. . . . Feel free to do that. . . . Remember, though, you can step out of the scene and back into your safe place at any time to stop, revise, and replay it. . . . You'll finally play the entire scenario through without stopping, seeing and hearing yourself give a superb performance . . . understanding that this brief exercise can represent a full-length interview. . . . If you become distracted at any time, simply refocus and continue.*

*Now begin . . . seeing yourself talking easily with one or more people . . . noting the environment, the temperature of the room, feeling genuinely supported . . . hearing the questions asked and your answers, given confidently as you enjoy the process . . . perhaps feeling drawn through the window into the scene . . . stepping out of the scene and using your remote control to stop and revise any part of the interview . . . playing the new scene with you feeling calm and confident . . . noting the interviewer's positive response to you . . . continuing the process of interviewing, revising, and replaying . . . and concluding the final scene.*

*Now, take the next minutes to replay selected portions of the interview through without stopping. . . . Simply hit the high points and mentally fast-forward through the rest. . . . You are a star performer giving a top interview performance. . . . Your subconscious is getting the message that you want complete success. . . . Allow the current scene to successfully conclude (record silence for thirty seconds or more).*

*Know that you've done your best . . . . Realize you have the skills to overcome challenges and that you'll be wiser and stronger for having done so. . . . You are able do whatever is needed to reach your goals.*

*Imagine yourself moving ahead in time to when you have the new position you want. . . . Sense it in as much detail as you can. . . . How will it feel to have successfully achieved your goal? Feel those feelings now . . . the satisfaction and accomplishment. . . . Allow it to sink deep within (record silence for thirty seconds).*

*In a moment, you will come back to full awareness of the room where your journey began, feeling relaxed and refreshed. . . The count of three, two, and one will help you return. . . . Three . . . begin to return, sense the feelings in your body . . . two, sense the environment around you and begin to move about . . . and one. . . . When you are ready, open your eyes and return, feeling awake and refreshed. Take a few slow, deep breaths, stretch if you like, and enjoy the moment.*

## Script: Meeting Your Mentor

Remember to begin your session with the Basic Relaxation Skills script.

*Finding yourself back in your safe place. . . . A slight movement out of the corner of your mental eye draws your attention and, as you look around, you notice someone waiting in the shadows at the edge of your safe place. . . . You nod in invitation, sensing it's not your Future Self this time and, as you approach one another, you become aware of a radiant light emanating from all around this being and wisdom in those eyes that seem to know you well. . . . Maybe you recognize this person. . . . Perhaps it's someone who has been a mentor or coach to you in the past—a relative perhaps, or a respected friend, living now or not. . . . Or perhaps it is someone you don't readily recognize. . . . Nevertheless, there is something familiar and comforting about those kind eyes and their powerful presence.*

*Welcome this Mentor into your safe place. . . . And, as you find a comfortable place to settle for a while, you may sit silently, being warmed in the supportive, loving presence. . . . Perhaps your Mentor will communicate with you through words . . . perhaps thoughts, images, or symbols . . . or some other unique way. . . . It doesn't matter. Simply drink it in. . . . You may use this time together for counsel and discussion of your current challenges and opportunities. . . . Perhaps you receive an assessment of the interviews you've mentally practiced, or other job search activities. . . . If advice is offered and it feels right to you, accept it with gratitude. . . . It's your choice. . . . (record silence for a minute or more).*

*Sense the beauty of your own life's journey from this new perspective, the magnificence of your own growth and development. . . . Perhaps you see a larger plan, new directions, and new opportunities. . . . Perhaps destiny is a choice after all. . . . And now, it's time to say goodbye. . . . As your Mentor departs, know that you may return here and meet again anytime you like.*

*In a moment you will come back to full awareness of the room where your journey began, feeling relaxed and refreshed. . . . The count of three, two, and one will help you return. . . . Three . . . begin to return, sense the feelings in your body . . . two, sense the environment around you, and begin to move around . . . and one. . . . When you are ready, open your eyes and return, feeling awake and refreshed. Take a few slow, deep breaths, stretch if you like, and enjoy the moment.*

# Appendix B

# Supplemental Exercises

## *Exercise 1: Recognizing Your Feelings*

This exercise is designed to help identify your specific feelings about your job loss. The script below will guide you through the experience.

Sit comfortably in a quiet location, safe from any disruption. In the exercise, you will set a clear intention to be rid of any distressing feelings. You will send that intention to your subconscious (your ally) by creating an image of surrounding those feelings in a translucent ball, identifying each of the feelings inside it, and tossing the ball away.

As with all the guided visualization scripts in this book, you may go through the exercise mentally as you read the words, or you may first read the script aloud into a recorder and then actually do the exercise while listening to it play.

Have your Journal nearby to use at the end of the exercise.

## *Script: Exercise 1*

*Find a comfortable position. . . . Gently close your eyes. Begin by focusing on your breathing—inhaling deeply . . . and exhaling fully. . . . Breathe deep into your diaphragm . . . breathing in relaxation . . . and breathing out any tension in your body. . . Inhale . . . exhale . . . relaxing more and more. . . . Imagine any distracting thoughts drifting away. . . . For the moment, your mind is still. . . . Feeling calm and relaxed now . . . inhaling deeply . . . and exhaling. . . . Allow these feelings of relaxation to spread through your body. . . . Notice the heaviness as your muscles begin to relax.*

*Imagine yourself in a very special and safe place where you can be alone and at peace. . . . You can create your safe place and change it any way you like, at any time. . . . Maybe it's a secluded place in nature, such as an ocean beach with gentle waves lapping at the shore, or a forest clearing with the soft sounds of birds . . . or perhaps a mountain meadow with a gentle breeze whispering through the wildflowers . . . any place where you feel comfortable and safe.*

*Look around your safe place. . . . Sense the shapes and colors coming into focus, becoming more and more clear. . . . Notice what time of day it is—perhaps the soft light of morning or the colorful setting sun. . . . Listen to the sounds of nature around you. . . . Notice the fragrance in the air. . . . Feel the earth under your feet, or run your fingers through the water that might be there.*

*Make yourself comfortable somewhere in your safe place. . . . Now let your attention drift to your job loss. . . . Allow your stressful feelings to surface without censoring them . . . all the discomforting feelings. . . . Notice where in your body they are located. . . . But don't dwell on them at this time. . . . Surround those feelings in a translucent ball by simply imagining a ball encircling all uncomfortable feelings.*

*Sense the ball holding your feelings move out of your body . . . and see it floating in the air in front of you. . . . Notice the feelings inside the ball and name those you can. . . . Others in your situation have felt fear, anxiety, shame, loneliness, anger, abandonment, and betrayal. . . . You may feel one or more of these emotions or something else entirely . . . and may find it difficult to distinguish between them. That's okay. . . . If you recognize anxiety, look deeper at what lies beneath it . . . perhaps a fear of failure or anger you don't think you should have.*

*Now take the ball and toss it away, perhaps only a few feet away or maybe high into the atmosphere. . . . Know in your heart and mind that you will soon be rid of these heavy feelings.*

*Take a couple of deep breaths and focus your attention back to your physical body and your environment. . . . When you're ready, open your eyes.*

Now, take your Journal and make a note of the different feelings you could identify within yourself.

---

## Exercise 2: Recognizing Future Possibilities

In this exercise, you'll imagine one of several possible paths for your life. Resist the urge to limit your happiness and accomplishments. Have some fun with the experience, and see what creative ideas begin to surface. One way to discover your own passion and potential is to look to those you admire. The abilities you envy in others are often the very talents inherent in you, waiting to be developed or discovered. Before you begin reading the exercise script, think of the people in your life and in the world whom you admire. Make a list of them. What is it you admire about each of them? What are the qualities you see that you'd like to have? In what arena are they successful? Is it one you're drawn to?

Next, read the script and follow the narrative instructions, or record it for playback. When you have completed the exercise with one of your imagined future selves, repeat it once or twice with other possible future selves. Imagine what your future might look like if you took a different career direction. For instance, if your first future self was a successful corporate executive, another future self may have become an entrepreneur, having developed an interest or skill into a financially successful business. What would that feel like? Explore your interests.

## *Script: Exercise 2*

*Sit comfortably in a quiet location where you won't be disturbed. . . . Imagine being once again in your place of relaxation and safety in nature . . . perhaps a garden with all your favorite flowers and trees . . . or an ocean beach, or a forest clearing. . . . It's a beautiful day, maybe sunrise or sunset . . . with the weather and temperature just as you like it . . . and you can hear the rustle of leaves or waves lapping at the shore. . . . Smell the fragrance in the air. . . . Make yourself comfortable somewhere in this relaxing place.*

*Now, think ahead to your own happy and success-filled future, maybe ten or more years from now. . . . Get a sense of what you look like, including your health and fitness. . . . What would you like your life to be like? . . . Are you doing work you love? . . . If so, what might it be? . . . Try and get a sense of your colleagues. . . . Or perhaps you are retired and enjoying all the things you never seemed to have time for before . . . family . . . travel . . . perhaps service projects. Who are the significant people in your life? . . . Sense your family—perhaps grown children—and friends around you. . . . What do you do for enjoyment in this future of yours? . . . Get a sense of the happiness and life satisfaction this future self is feeling. . . . Take as much time as you like.*

*When you're ready, come back to full awareness of the room where your journey began. . . . Take a few slow, deep breaths, and enjoy the moment.*

When you have completed the exercise two or three times, determine which of the futures you feel most drawn to. Then, explore it further and in greater depth, without a script. As you do, notice how deep your desire is for that future, and ask yourself if you actually believe it's possible and if you expect it to happen. Allow yourself to explore dreams and possibilities. (Later you can consider the practical questions about what it would take to prepare for and create that future.)

In your Journal, jot down your feelings and observations after each future-self experience. Which future were you most drawn to, and why? What fears or anxieties came up?

---

## Exercise 3: Refining Your Visualization Skills

If guided visualization is brand new to you, I'd like to share a few brief exercises designed to sharpen your imagery skills. The Job-Loss Recovery Program will be of greater benefit if you work with these exercises before implementing Module 1.

Intimate involvement in the guided visualization program scenarios is of paramount importance for optimal success. Remember, even if your predominant sense is not visual, visualization can still have power and depth when you engage all five senses. To demonstrate, try the following quick exercise. In the process, you will be improving your imagery and visualization skills. Read through it once to get the idea, and then close your eyes and walk through the scenario.

## Script: Exercise 3

*First, get comfortable in your chair and take a deep breath. . . . Imagine yourself in your kitchen, standing over a cutting board, holding a sharp knife. . . . In your mind's eye, see a juicy lemon sitting on the cutting board. . . . Notice the yellow color and the shape. . . . Take the lemon in your mental hand. Feel the temperature, the weight, and smell the fragrance. . . . Place it back on the board and pick up the knife. . . . Cut the lemon in half and notice the sections of lemon and rind. . . . Cut it in half again, hearing the knife thump the cutting board. . . . Notice the seeds, the juice, and the scent. . . . Bring a lemon slice to your mouth and bite down. Suck the sour lemon juice and swallow it.*

Salivation is ruled by the autonomic nervous system and is normally out of conscious control. If you salivated when you mentally swallowed the lemon juice, then your own body was tricked, in a sense, into believing you were sucking an actual lemon.

---

Another exercise to enhance clarity and focus is to simply go to your safe place and practice using all your senses. For instance, you could feel the mist of dawn on your face as you watch the sun come up over the horizon. If there's a lake nearby, you might take a swim or a sail in the breeze. Smell blooming lilacs, pine trees, ocean air, or any of your favorite smells. Listen to melodic birdcalls, whistling wind in the trees, or a foghorn in the distance. Play an instrument you enjoy playing or have always wanted to play. Feel the rough bark of a tree, a velvety flower petal, or gritty sand under your feet. Pick up a kitten or puppy, and feel the softness and warmth as you pet it. Imagine eating some of your favorite foods.

In *The Mental Edge* (1999), Kenneth Baum recommends the use of six imaginary knobs to enhance visualization. Here's how it works: To begin, think of an exciting and satisfying time you've experienced. For example, you could think back to when you received a job offer you had really wanted, or to a time when you played the best game of your life at your favorite sport. See yourself going through the motions of that event, and allow yourself to feel the exhilaration of the moment.

Now imagine there are six knobs in front of you. One is a zoom lens to make your internal picture larger, one is to enhance the color, and another is to add brightness to your picture. The others control volume, tone, and fine-tuning of the sound. Experiment with them to make your images more clear, detailed, and three-dimensional.

Yet another effective exercise to refine your imaging skills entails sitting comfortably and picking out an object in the room. Look at it and study it intensely—the shape, size, color, and details. Now close your eyes and try to replicate it in your mind's eye. Open your eyes and fill in the details you may have missed. Try it again with another object of a different shape and color. Try this daily or before every guided visualization session.

Have fun with these exercises. Experiment to see what you find most engaging and what is most challenging. Practice even more to develop and strengthen your less dominant senses.

# Appendix C

# References

Achterberg, J., C. Kenner, and G. F. Lawlis. 1988. Severe burn injury: A comparison of relaxation, imagery and biofeedback for pain management. *Journal of Mental Imagery* 12:71-88.

Baum, K., and R. Turbo. 1999. *The Mental Edge.* Berkeley, CA: Berkley Publishing Group.

Birkel, J. D., and S. J. Miller. 1998. *Career Bounce-Back!: The Professionals in Transition Guide to Recovery and Reemployment.* Boston: AMACOM.

Dolbee, S. 2001. Peace proposal: Forgiveness may be the path to healing. *The San Diego Union-Tribune,* April 15.

Fanning, Patrick. 1994. *Visualization for Change.* Oakland, CA: New Harbinger Publications.

Jacobson, E. 1938. *Progressive Relaxation.* Chicago: University of Chicago Press.

Johnson, S. 1998. *Who Moved My Cheese?: An Amazing Way to Deal with Change in Your Work and in Your Life.* New York: G. P. Putnam's Sons.

Joseph, L. M. 2009. *The Job-Loss Recovery Program: The Ultimate Visualization System for Landing a Great Job Now!* (Compact Disc) Riverside, CA: Discovery Dynamics, Inc.

Joseph, L. M., and M. A. Greenberg. 2001. The effects of a career transition program on reemployment success in laid-off professionals. *Consulting Psychology Journal* 53:169-181.

Kubler-Ross, Elisabeth. 1969, 1997. *On Death and Dying.* New York: Simon & Schuster.

Morel, L. 2009. *Get Clear. Get Connected. Get a Job.* Santa Monica, CA: Beyond Words Group, Inc.

Naparstek, B. 1994. *Staying Well with Guided Imagery: How to Harness the Power of Your Imagination for Health and Healing.* NewYork: Warner Books.

Nicklaus, J., and K. Bowden. 1998. *Golf My Way.* New York: Simon & Schuster.

Orlick, T. 1990. *In Pursuit of Excellence: How to Win in Sport and Life through Mental Training.* Champaign, IL: Human Kinetics.

Overholser, J. C. 1990. Passive relaxation training with guided imagery: A transcript for clinical use. *Phobia Practice and Research Journal* 3:107-122.

Peale, N. V. 1982. *Positive Imaging: The Powerful Way to Change Your Life.* New York: Fawcett Columbine.

_____. 1952, 1996. *The Power of Positive Thinking.* New York: Ballantine Books.

Pert, C. B. 1997. *Molecules of Emotion: Why You Feel the Way You Feel.* New York: Scribner.

Price, R. H., Choi, J. N, and Vinokur, A. D. 2002. Links in the Chain of Adversity Following Job Loss: How Financial Strain and Loss of Personal Control Lead to Depression, Impaired Functioning, and Poor Health. *Journal of Occupational Health Psychology* 7:4.

Rossman, M. 2000. *Guided Imagery for Self-Healing.* Tiburon, CA: H. J. Kramer.

Ruvolo, A. P., and H. R. Markus. 1992. Possible selves and performance: The power of self-relevant imagery. *Social Cognition* 10:95-124.

Sher, B. 1994. *How to Live the Life You Love.* Audiocassettes. New York: Bantam Doubleday. Barbara Sher Tapes.

Smith, D. 1990. Imagery in sport: An historical and current overview. In *Mental Imagery*, edited by R. Kunzendorf. New York: Plenum Press.

Spera, S. P., E. D. Buhrfeind, and J. W. Pennebaker. 1994. Expressive writing and coping with job loss. *Academy of Management Journal* 37:722-733.

Tracy, B. 2002. *Create Your Own Future: How to Master the 12 Critical Factors of Unlimited Success.* New York: John Wiley and Sons.

Ungerleider, S. 1996. *Mental Training for Peak Performance: Top Athletes Reveal the Mind Exercises They Use to Excel.* Emmaus, PA: Rodale Press.

Ungerleider, S., and J. M. Golding. 1991. Mental practice among Olympic athletes. *Perceptual and Motor Skills* 72:1007-1017.

Witkin, Georgia. 2002. *Stress-Relief for Disasters Great and Small.* New York: Newmarket Press.

# About the Author

Lynn Joseph, Ph.D., Psychologist and Career and Life Transition Specialist, is a leading authority on the use of guided visualization techniques to bounce back from job loss. Her mission is to provide innovative tools that help others reduce stress and elegantly achieve their goals despite obstacles and setbacks.

She formerly served as SVP, Career & Life Transition Programs, Parachute, Inc., and was previously an executive search consultant. She also worked with Fortune 100 companies Johnson & Johnson, and Abbott Laboratories in the arenas of sales management, training, and human resources.

Dr. Joseph has studied the development and application of guided visualization technology for twenty-five years, and has used the techniques to enhance her own life as well as others'. Her landmark study--that used visualization techniques to significantly reduce the landing time of dislocated workers--was published in the *Consulting Psychology Journal*, a peer-reviewed journal of the American Psychological Association. Its Job-Loss Recovery Program was endorsed by the Substance Abuse and Mental Health Services Administration (SAMHSA), U.S. Dept. of Health and Human Services.

Dr. Joseph has been featured on hundreds of radio and TV programs and quoted in such publications as *Time* and *Fortune* Magazines and the *Washington Post*. Visit www.DrLynnJoseph.com.

She lives in the Los Angeles area with her husband and their two cats and two dogs.

# Some Other Discovery Dynamics, Inc. Titles

*The Job-Loss Recovery Program: The Ultimate Visualization System for Landing a Great Job Now!* (Compact Disc) $17.98

This is an audio CD of *The Job-Loss Recovery Program Guide*'s guided visualization exercises (Modules 1 and 2). It includes the complete program, narrated in the soothing voice of Dr. Lynn Joseph and accompanied by Grammy-nominated Celtic Harpist Lisa Lynne. Also available in mp3 format.

*The Job-Loss Recovery Program: Supplemental Guided Exercises* (Compact Disc) $13.95

This is an audio CD of the supplemental guided visualization exercises that appear in Chapter 9 and Appendix B of *The Job-Loss Recovery Program Guide*. Dr. Joseph narrates, accompanied by Celtic Harpist Lisa Lynne.

*Emotional Renewal Guided Imagery for Caregivers: Looking After Yourself While Helping a Loved One* (Compact Disc) $17.98

This is an all new audio CD by Dr. Lynn Joseph, accompanied by Celtic harpist Lisa Lynne. Seven guided visualization exercises lead the listener beyond the challenges and stresses of caring for a loved one to a place of inner calm and peaceful resolution with greater self-care. It is a valuable tool for family caregivers, family caregiver counselors and other support professionals. Listen and take back control of your time! Also available in mp3 format.

Call toll free, 1-888-557-7776, or visit our online store at www.discoverydynamics.net for more information and to order.

Prices subject to change without notice.

Printed in the United States
150901LV00003B/1/P